GREGG SHORTHAND

Manual for the
Functional Method

by

Louis A. Leslie, C.S.R.

Arranged in accordance with the
Anniversary Edition of Gregg Shorthand

THE GREGG PUBLISHING COMPANY

New York   Chicago   Boston   San Francisco

Toronto   London   Sydney

PRINTED IN THE UNITED STATES OF AMERICA

CHAPTER VIII

ASSIGNMENT 40

196. Drill on Previous Assignments

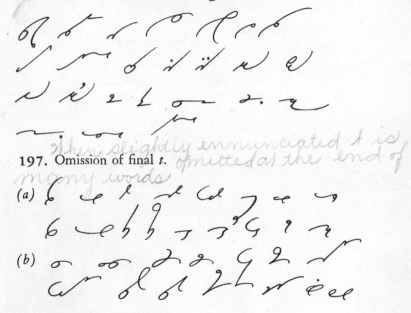

197. Omission of final *t.*

When slightly enunuciated t is omitted at the end of many words

(a)

(b)

198. The final *t* must be written in some words.

199. Reading and Writing Exercise

Choices

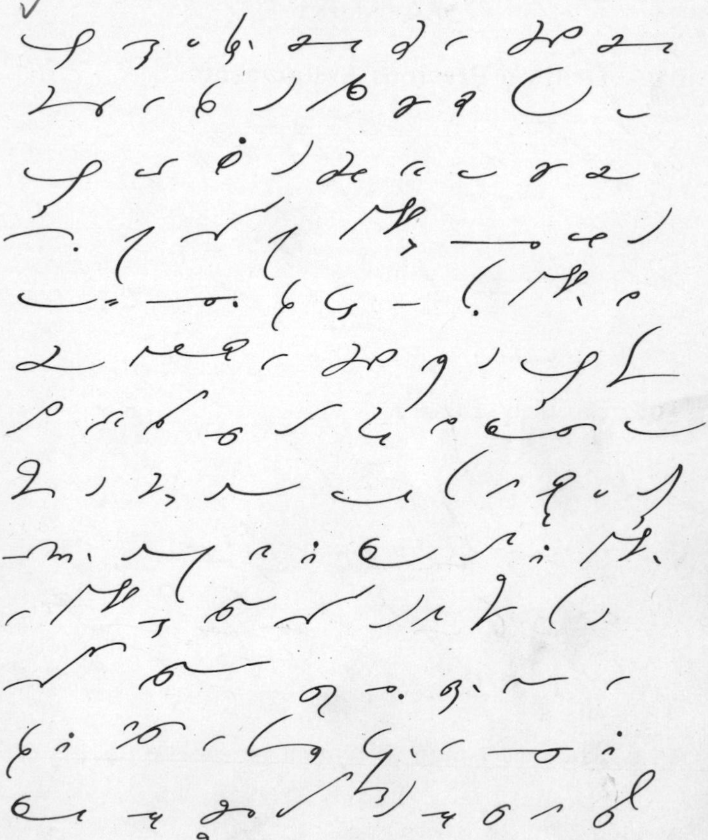

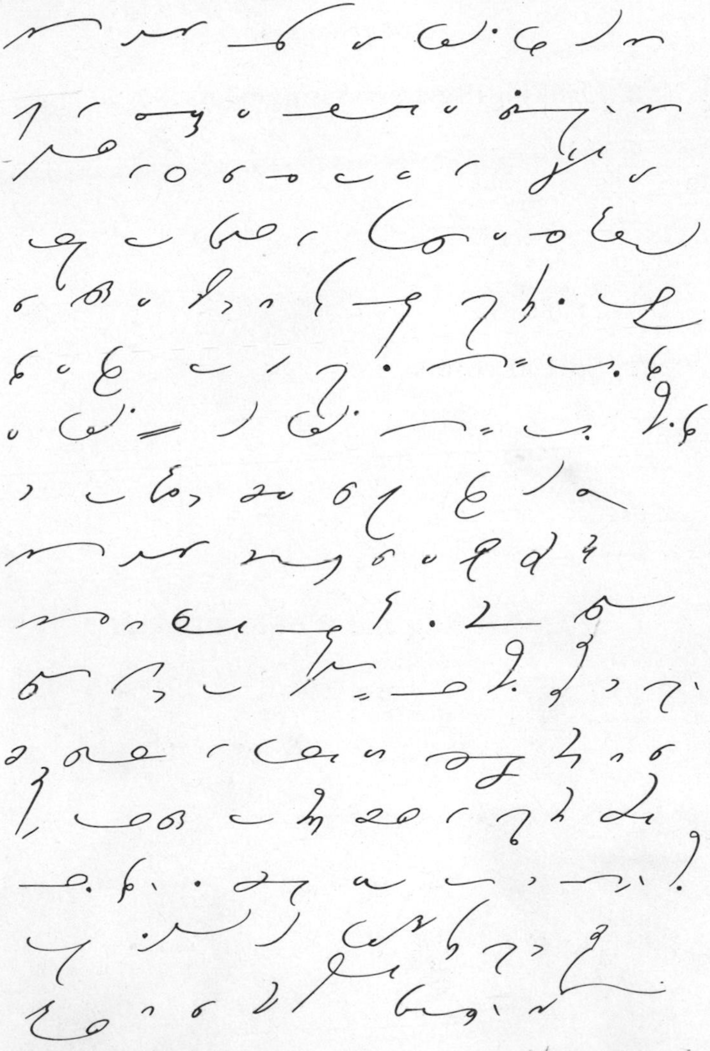

Assignment 41

200. Drill on Previous Assignments

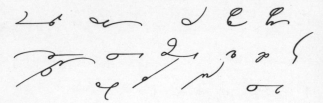

201. Special Forms

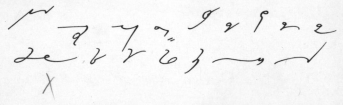

202. Reading and Writing Exercise

Waste Land

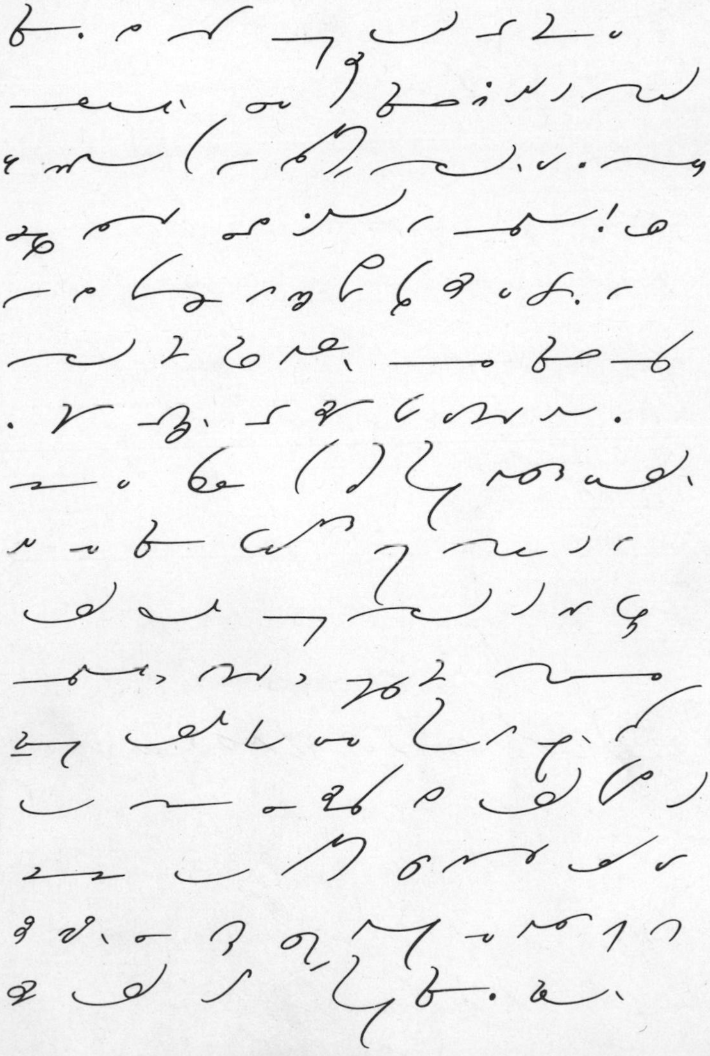

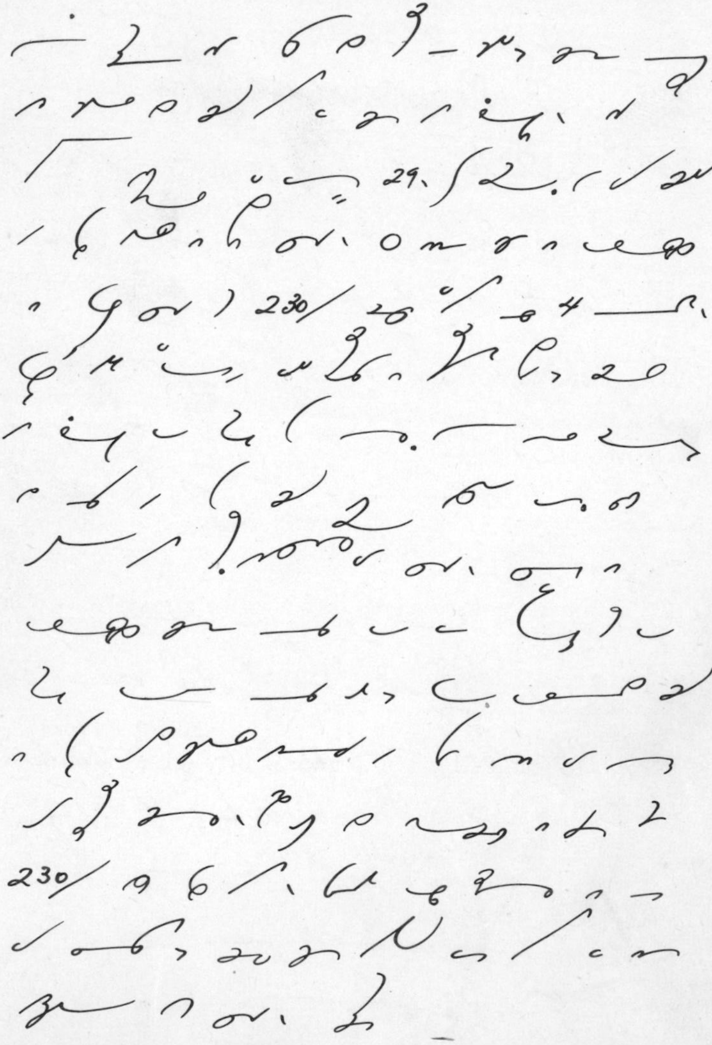

ASSIGNMENT 42

203. Drill on Previous Assignments

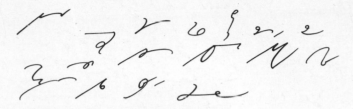

204. Omission of final *d*.

205. There are three words in which the *d* must be written.

206. *D* is omitted when it immediately precedes *m* or *v*.

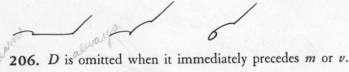

207. Special Forms

208. Prefixes and Suffixes

(a) 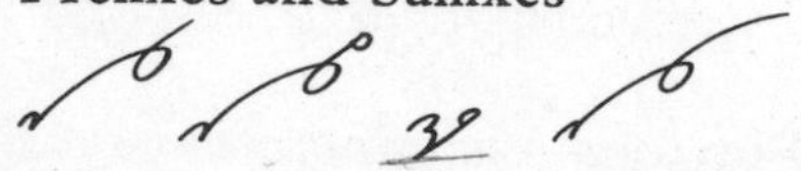

(b) 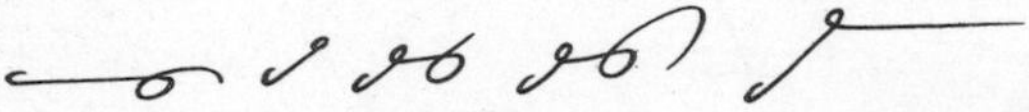

(c) 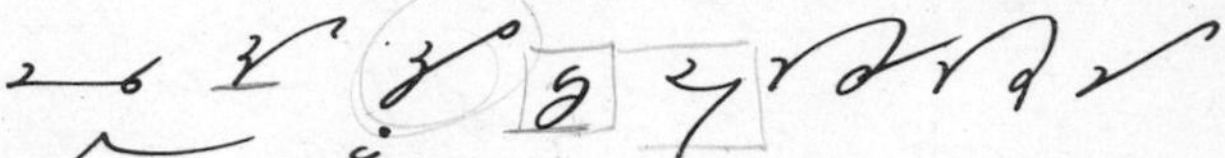

(d) 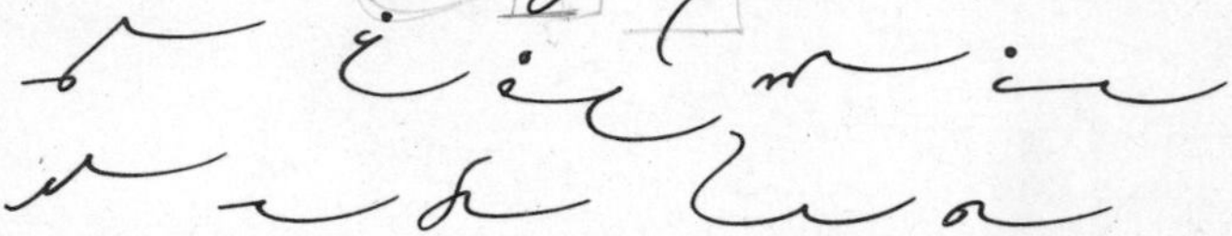

209. Reading and Writing Exercise

A RACE WITH THE CLOCK

Before r, l, c, h, ch, g or a hook sub is written contrary to the rule to express sub.

ASSIGNMENT 43

210. Drill on Previous Assignments

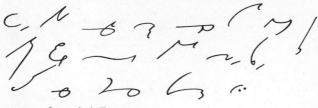

211. Special Forms

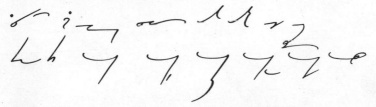

212. Reading and Writing Exercise

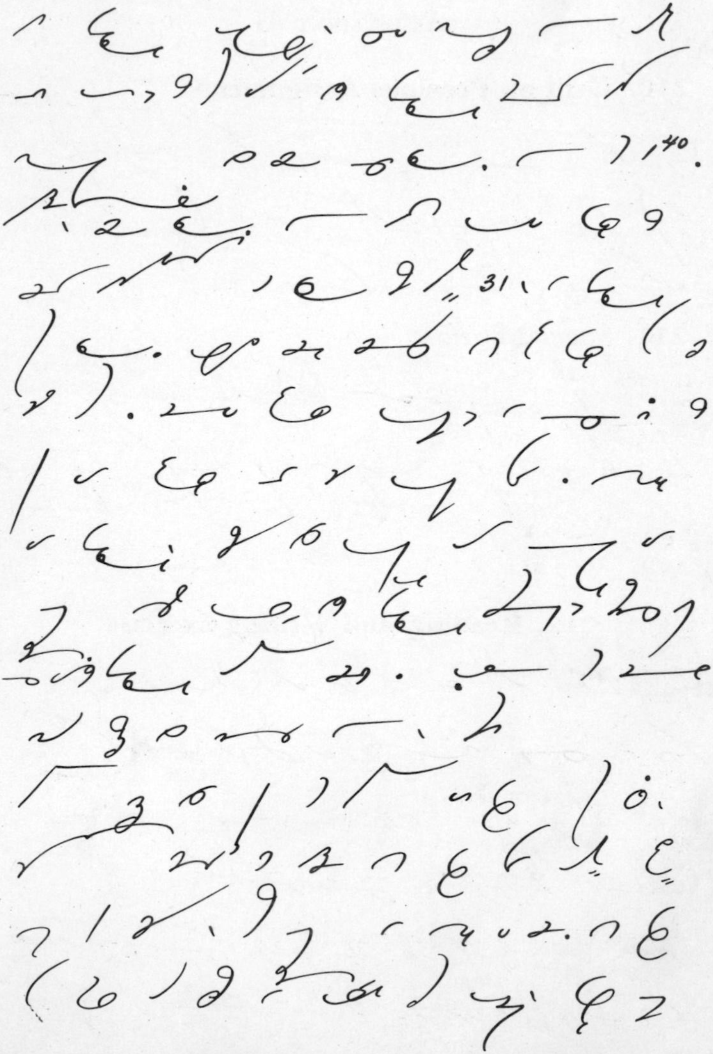

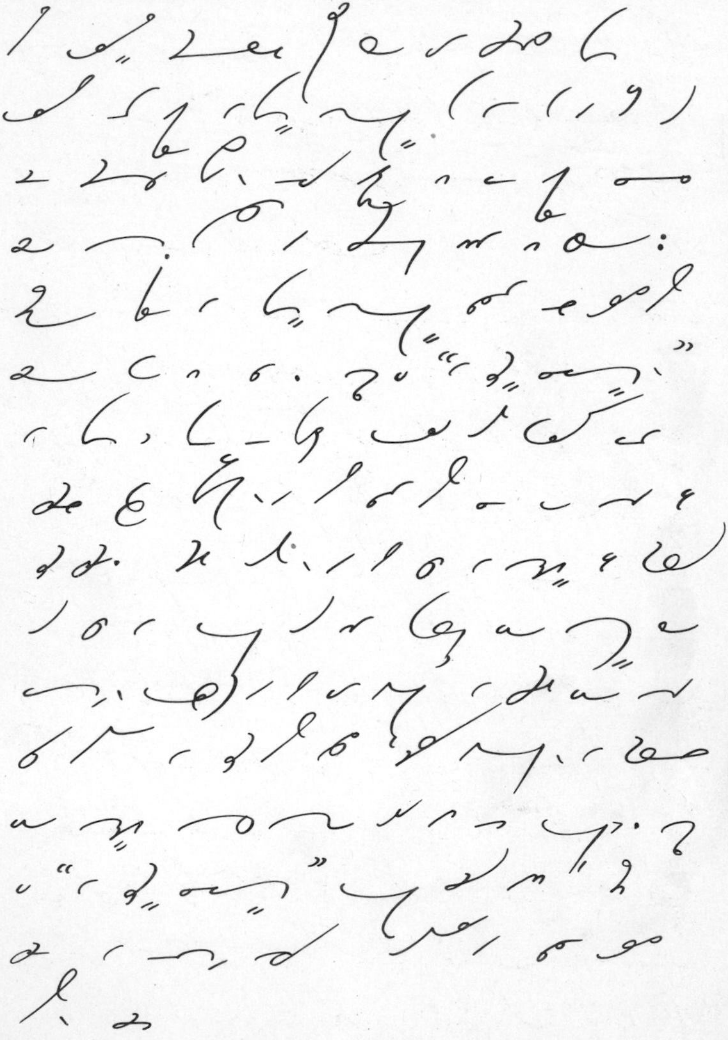

Assignment 44

213. Drill on Previous Assignments

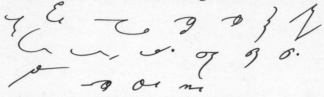

214. Any unimportant word may be omitted where the sense requires its restoration in transcribing.

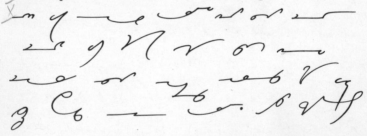

215. Reading and Writing Exercise

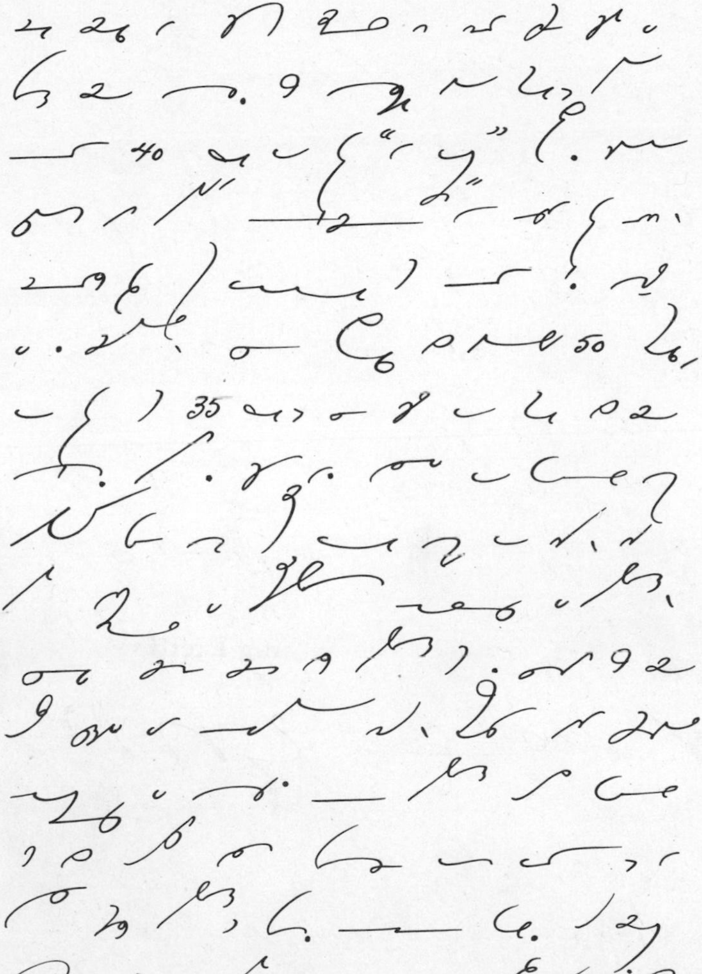

Assignment 45

216. Drill on Previous Assignments

217. Special Forms

218. Reading and Writing Exercise

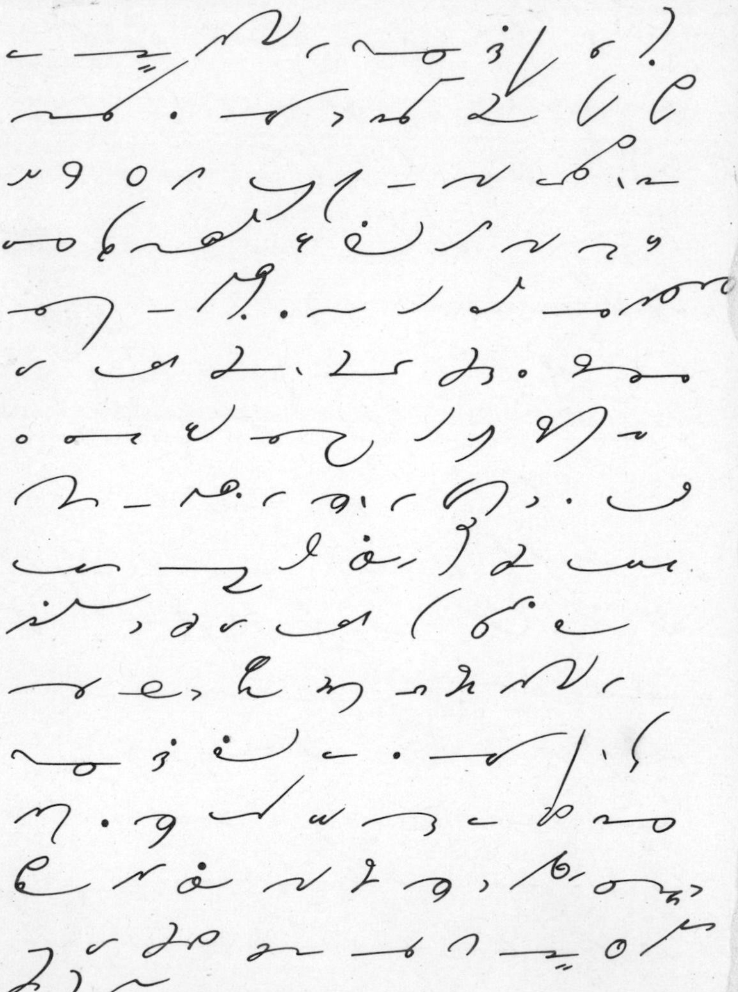

CHAPTER IX

ASSIGNMENT 46

219. Drill on Previous Assignments

write

220. Special Forms

221. Special Forms Similar to Longhand Abbreviations

222. Reading and Writing Exercise

A Trip to Mexico

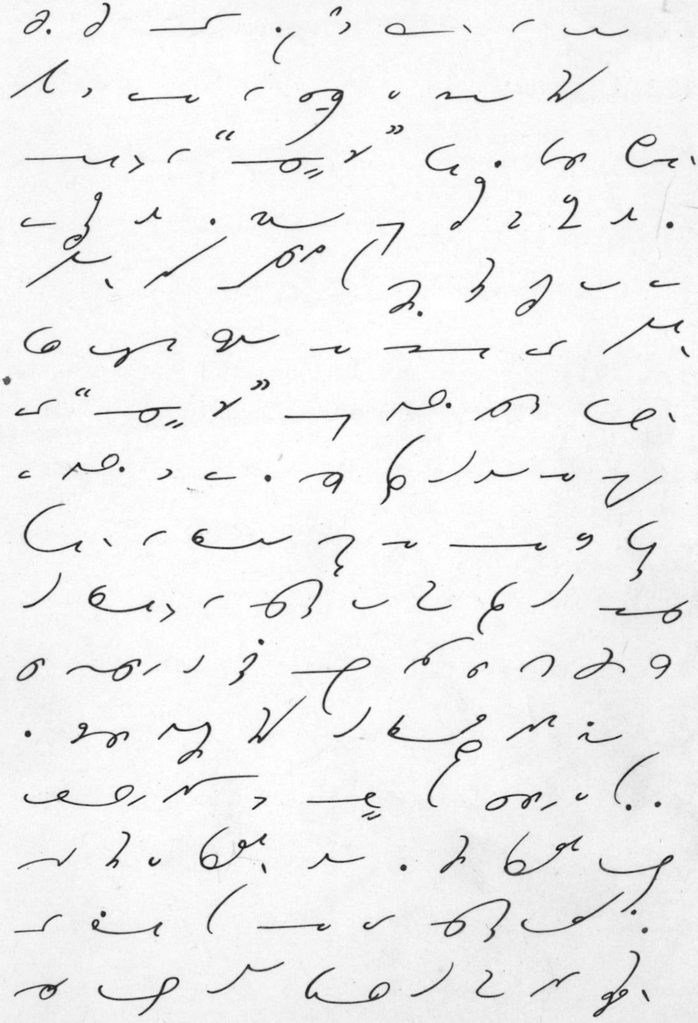

ASSIGNMENT 47

223. Drill on Previous Assignments

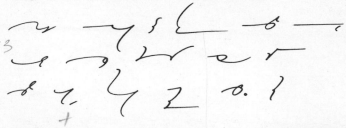

224. Many long words may be abbreviated by dropping the terminations. This principle is already familiar in longhand, as *Rev.* for *Reverend; Phila.* for *Philadelphia.* The extent to which this abbreviating principle may be applied depends upon the familiarity of the writer with the words and subject matter.

225. Special Forms

226. Reading and Writing Exercise

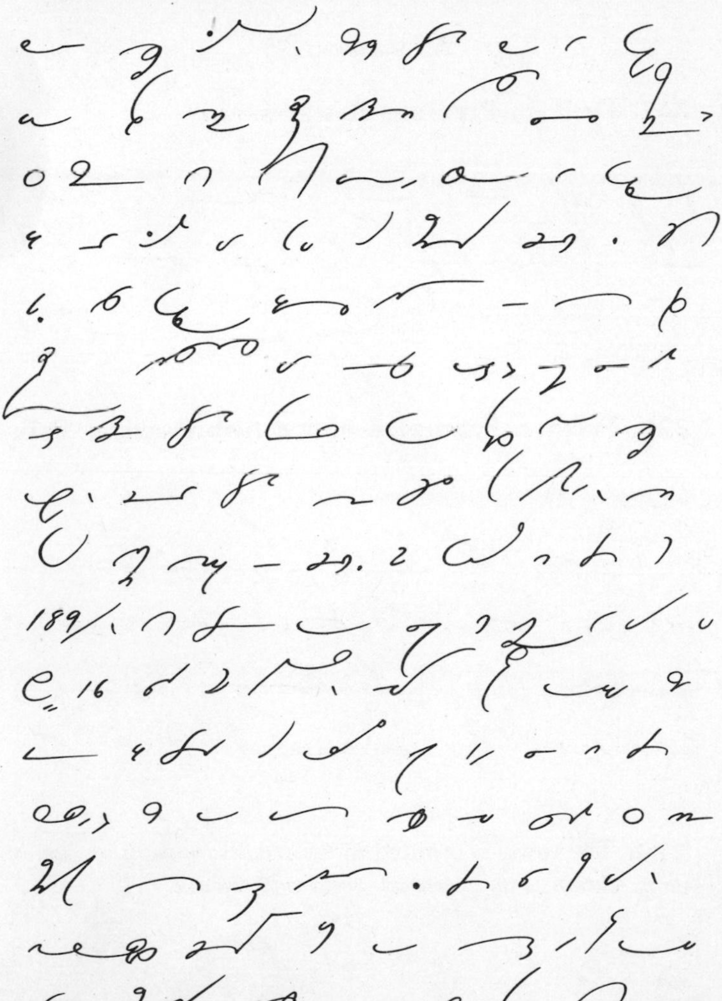

Assignment 48

227. Drill on Previous Assignments

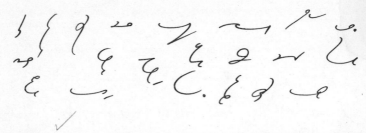

228. Further Examples of the Abbreviating Principle

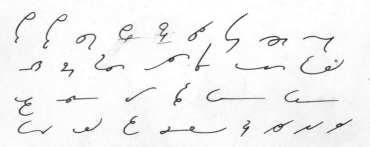

229. The vowel is omitted in the terminations *tition, tation, dition, dation, nition, nation, mission, mation.*

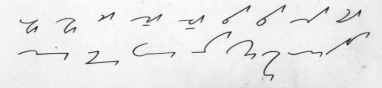

230. Reading and Writing Exercise

Timepieces

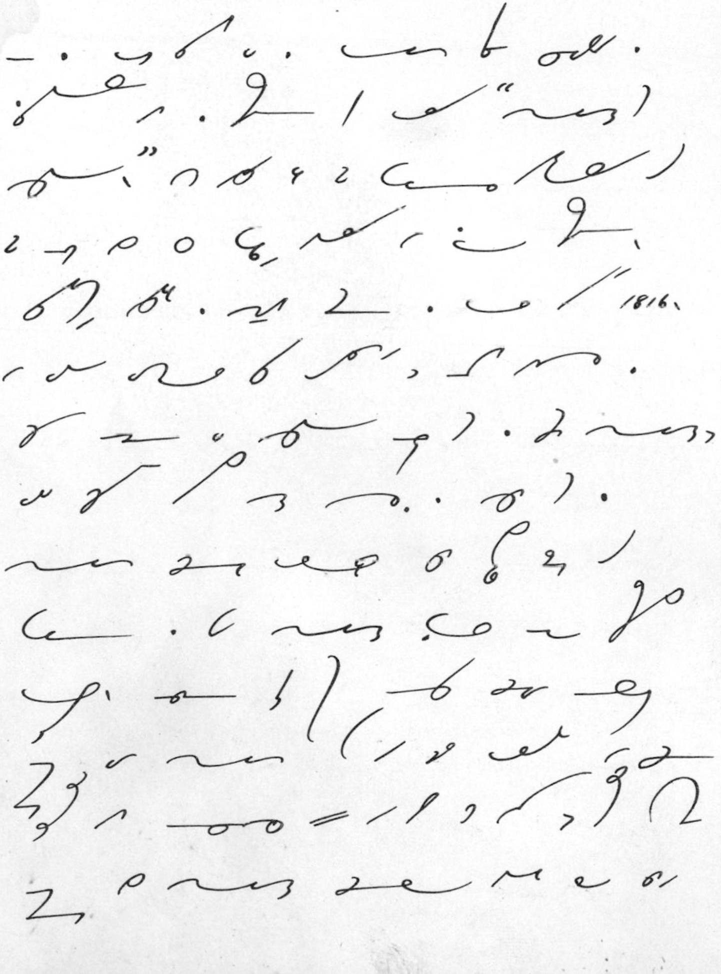

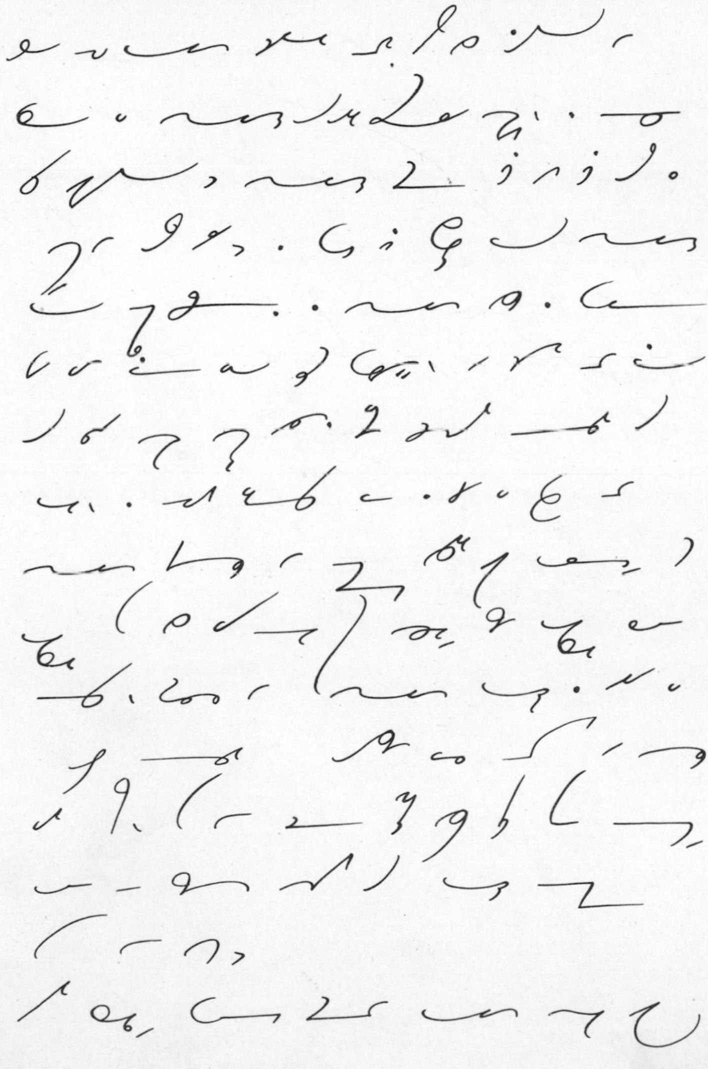

ASSIGNMENT 49

231. Drill on Previous Assignments

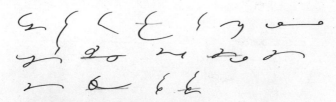

232. Special Forms

233. Brief-Form Derivatives

Any:

Be:

Ever-y:

Here:

There:

a compound word is a word made up of two or more simple words

234. Reading and Writing Exercise

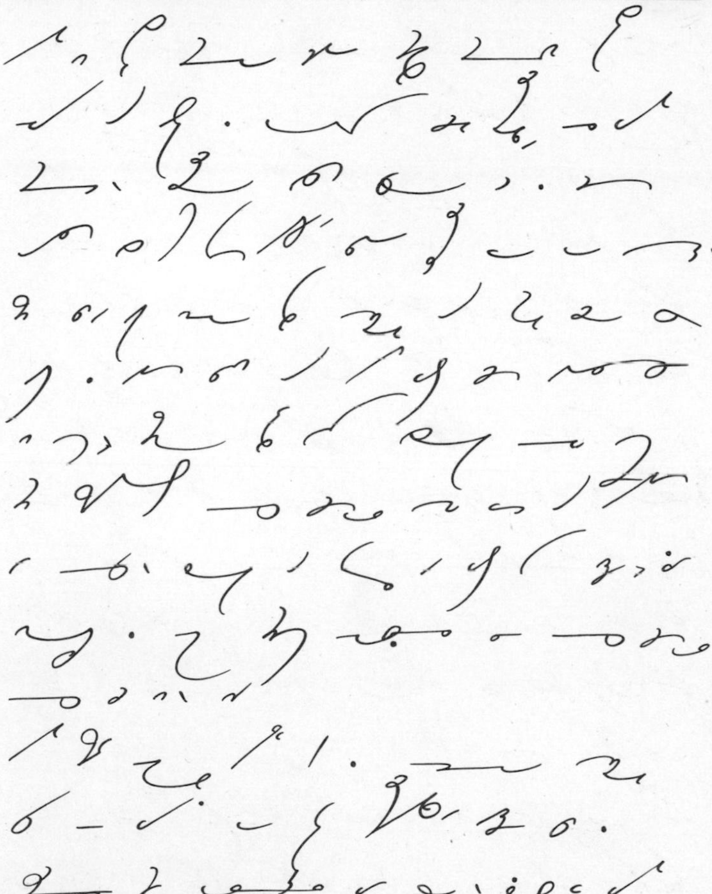

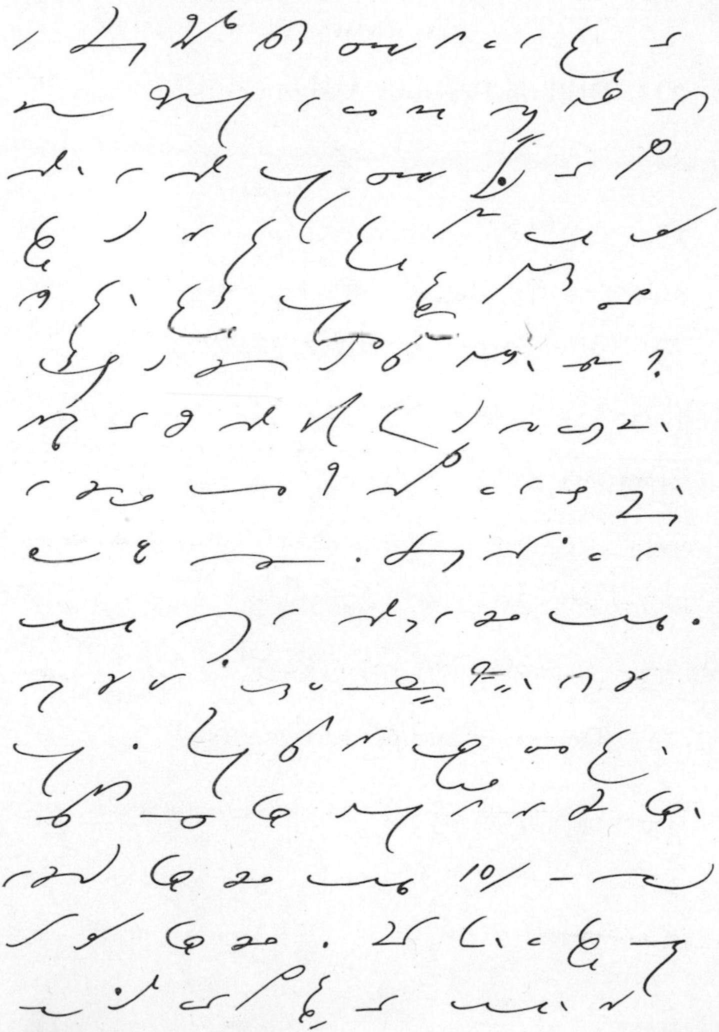

ASSIGNMENT 50

235. Drill on Previous Assignments

236. Brief-Form Derivatives. *(Continued.)*

Where:

Soever:

Some:

With:

237. Quantities and Measurements

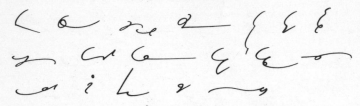

238. Reading and Writing Exercise

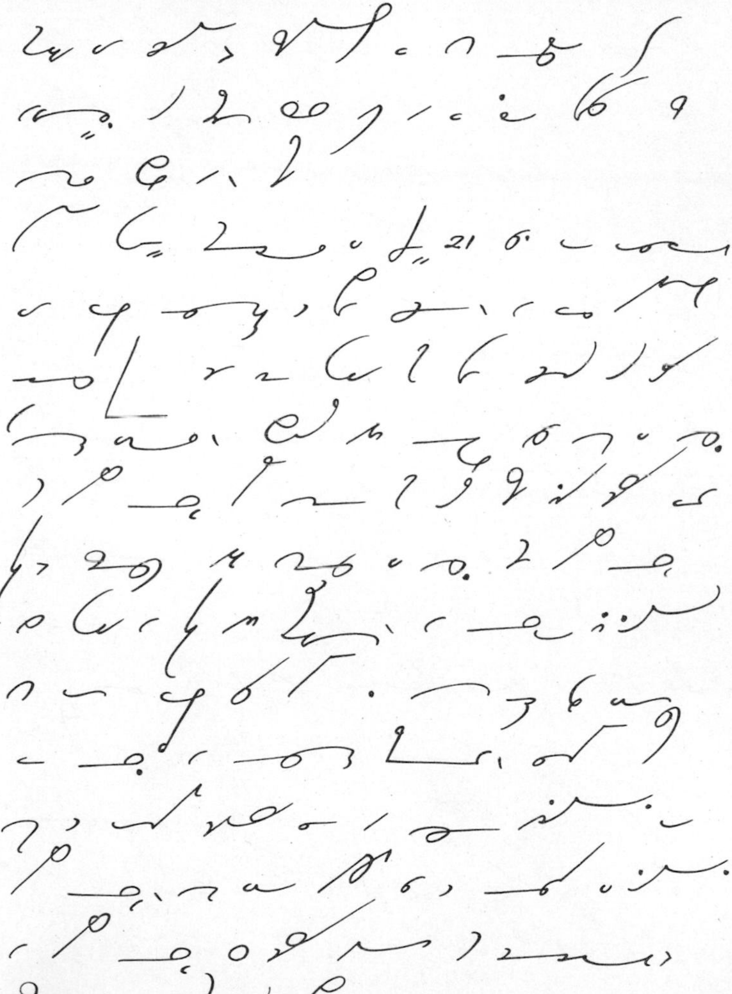

Assignment 51

239. Drill on Previous Assignments

these

240. The *s* for *cents* is placed in the position ordinarily occupied by the small figures used to express *cents*.

241. Special Forms

242. Reading and Writing Exercise

CHAPTER X

243. Drill on Previous Assignments

244. In forming the derivatives of words ending in *ct*, as in *contact*, a final *or, er, ed, ive* may be joined.

245. The word *done* is expressed by the *den* blend in many phrases.

246. In many phrases, the word *than* is expressed by *n*.

247. The form for *us* is often modified in phrases.

248. In many phrases, *department* is expressed by a disjoined *d*.

249. Reading and Writing Exercise

Assignment 53

250. Drill on Previous Assignments

251. Special Phrases

252. Many useful phrases may be formed by writing one character through another.

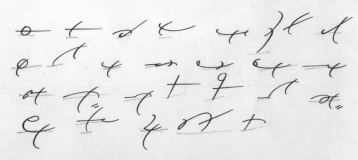

253. Reading and Writing Exercise

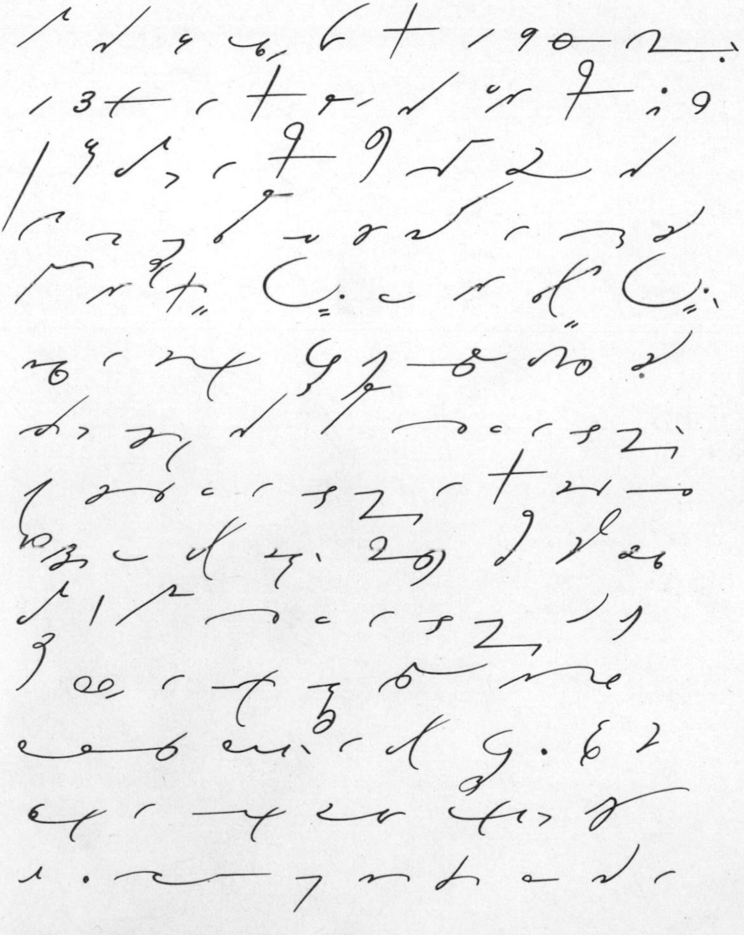

Wed - Thur.

254. Drill on Previous Assignments

[shorthand outlines]

Jr. Principal.

255. Incl- *is expressed by a small circle placed above the line.*

[shorthand outlines]

✓ 256. -ciency- *cient + tient are expressed by tion - t / ✓*

[shorthand outlines]

✓ 257. -ship *is expressed by sh in the ing position.*

[shorthand outlines]

258. Post- *is expressed by p on the*

[shorthand outlines]

259. Circu- *sely, sircum are ex-*
pressed by disjoined backward s

[shorthand outlines]

placed above the line.

260. Intr- *inter- enter or intel ex-*
pressed by n placed above the line

[shorthand outlines]

n above the line +
b " " " " "

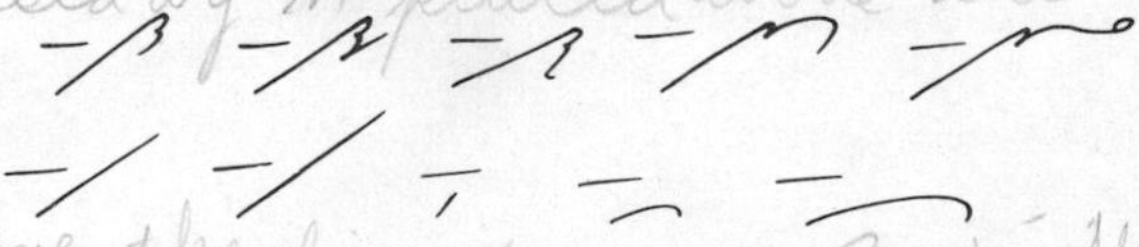

Reading and Writing Exercise

261. *[shorthand outlines]*

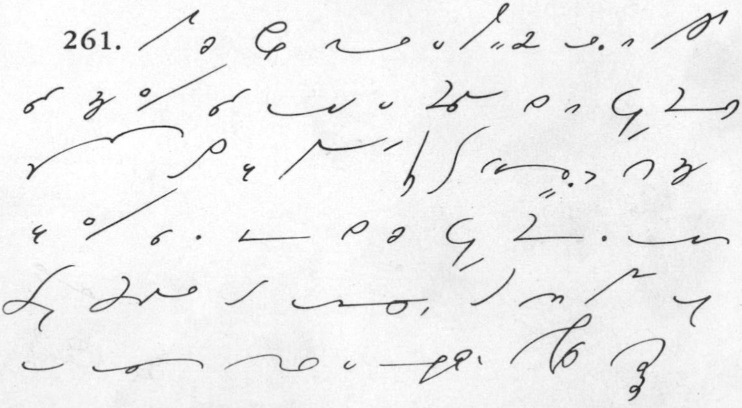

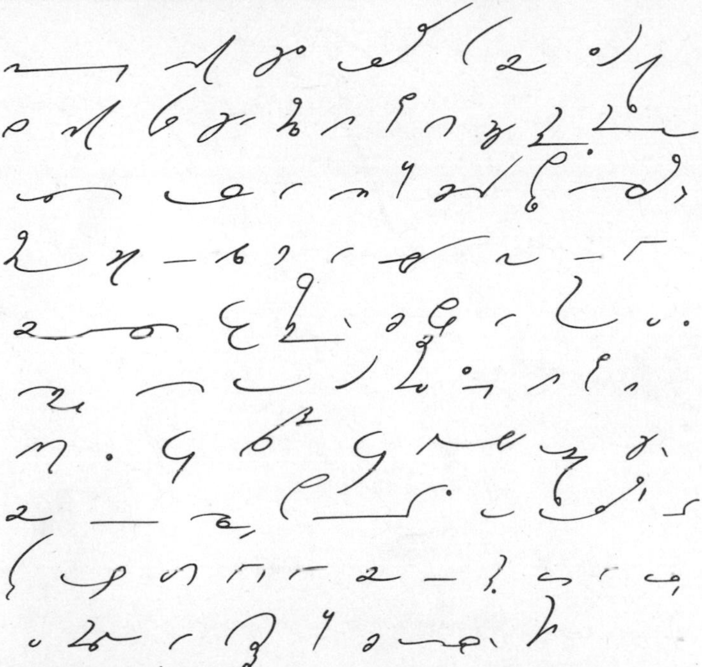

262.

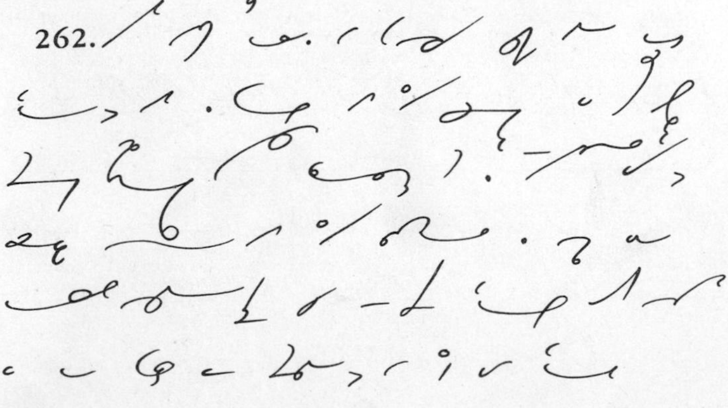

263.

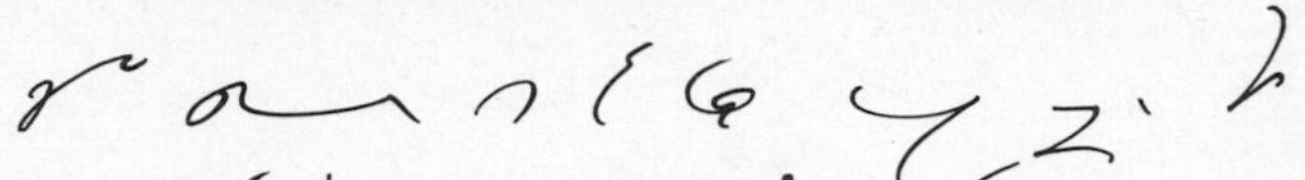

264.

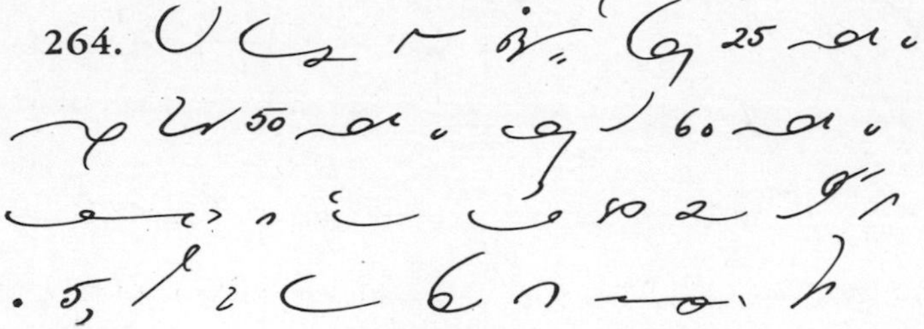

265. Relax

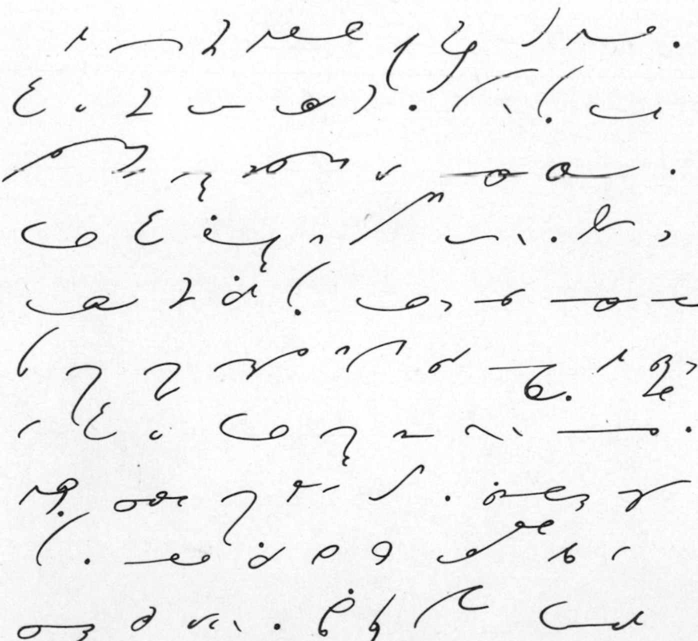

Assignment 55 *Tues.*

266. Drill on Previous Assignments

267. Inter- *enter or intel by disjoined n placed above the line*

268. Distr- *+ destra by ds disjoined + placed above the line*

269. Centr- *center – sn – above the line*

270. Short-, ship- *by disjoined ish placed above the line*

[shorthand outlines]

Reading and Writing Exercise *write 7*

271.

[shorthand outlines]

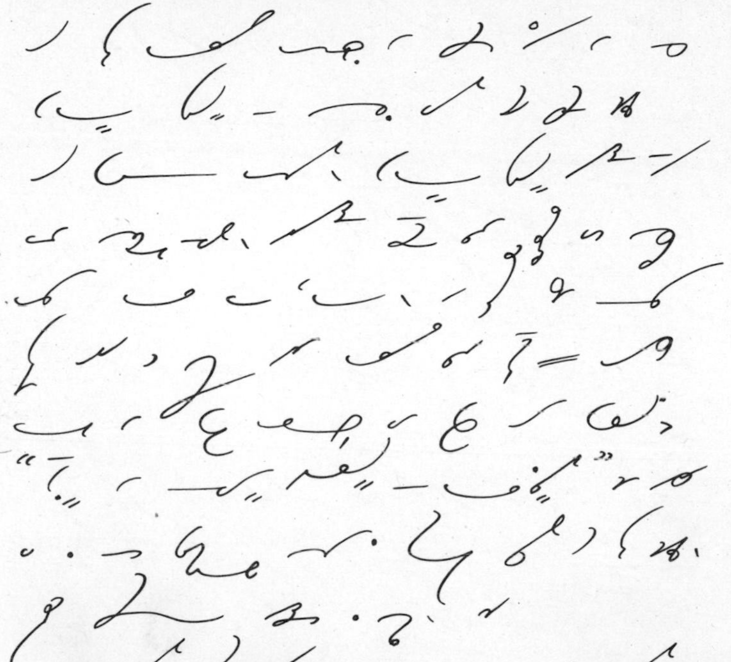

272.

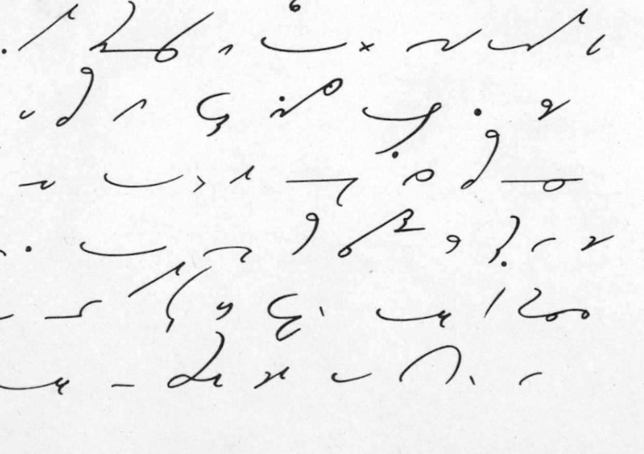

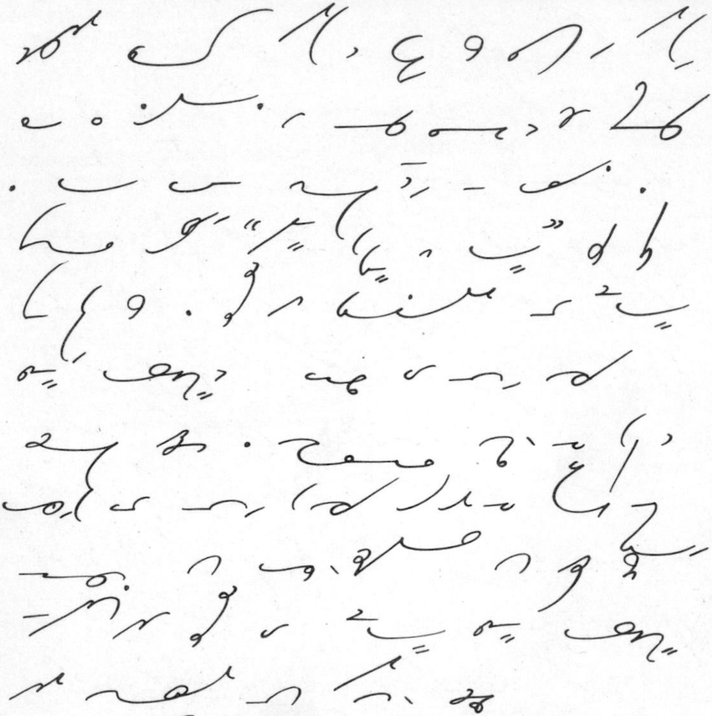

273.

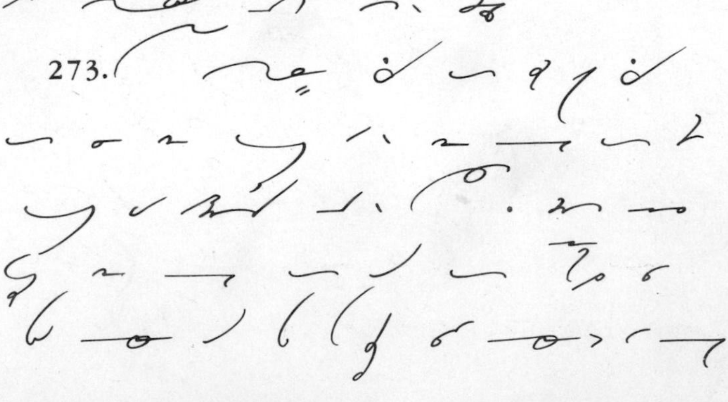

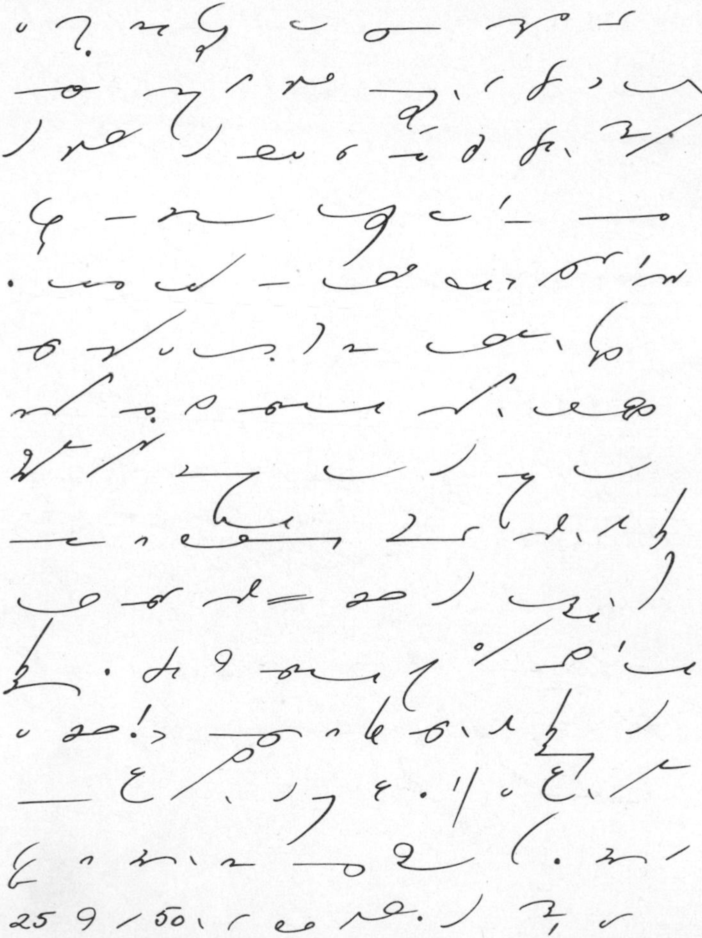

274. *(shorthand outlines)*

231

275. *(shorthand outlines)*

24 25

ASSIGNMENT 56

276. Drill on Previous Assignments

277. Under- *upper hook above the line*

278. Over- *by lower hook above the line*

279. Aggr- *aggr – expressed by loop above the line*

280. Para- *by p above the line*

281. Contr- *by k-above the line.*

Reading and Writing Exercise

282.

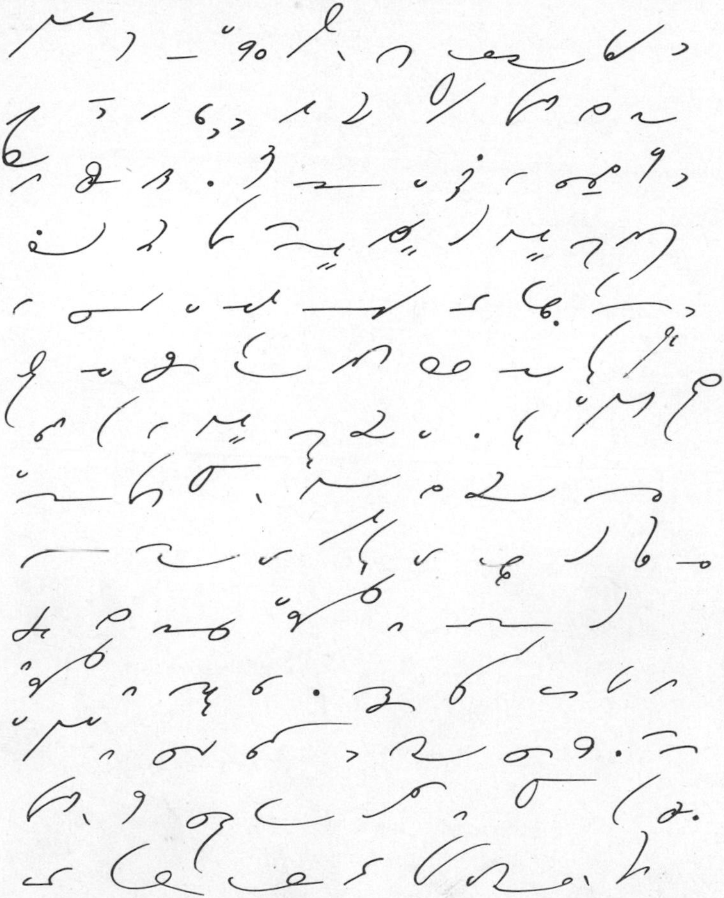

283.

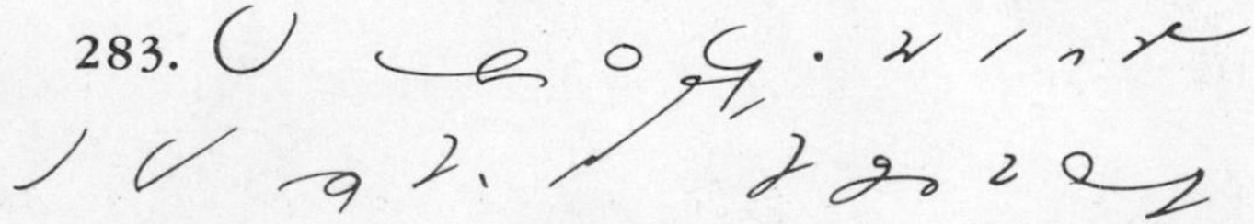

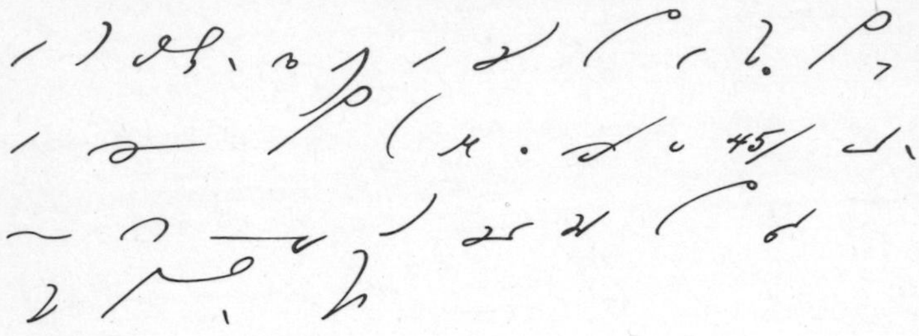

284.

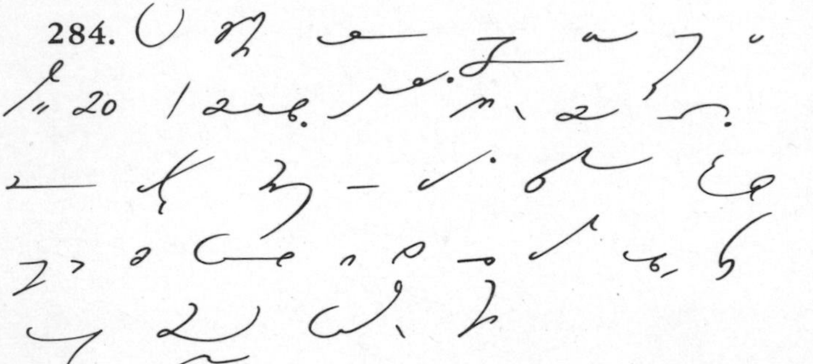

285.

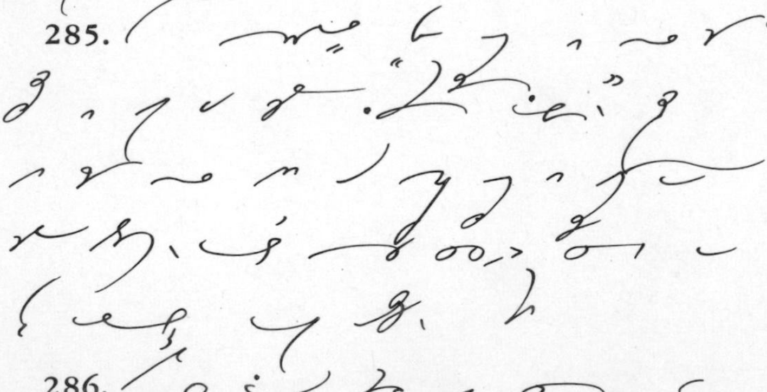

286.

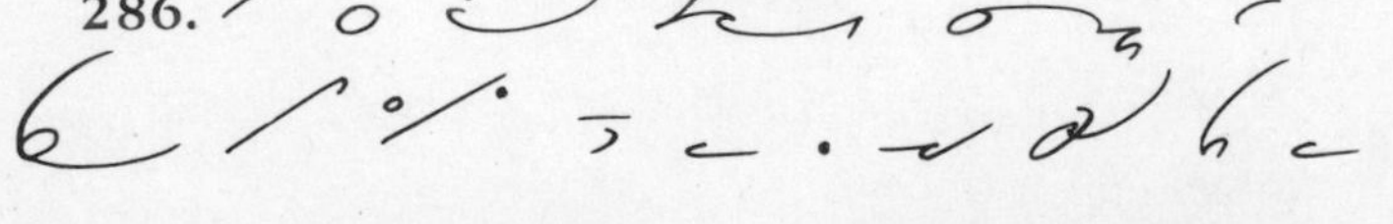

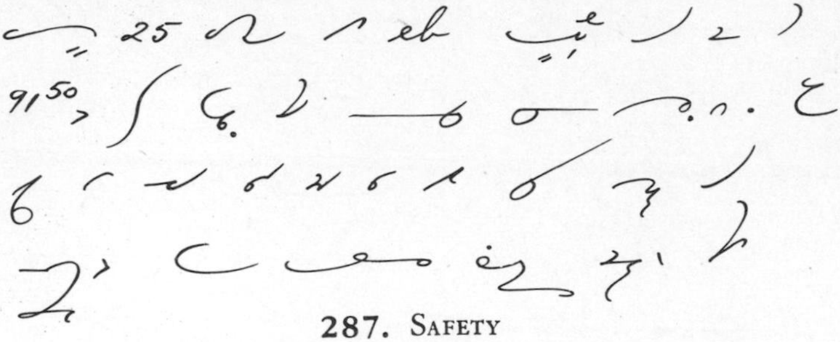

287. Safety

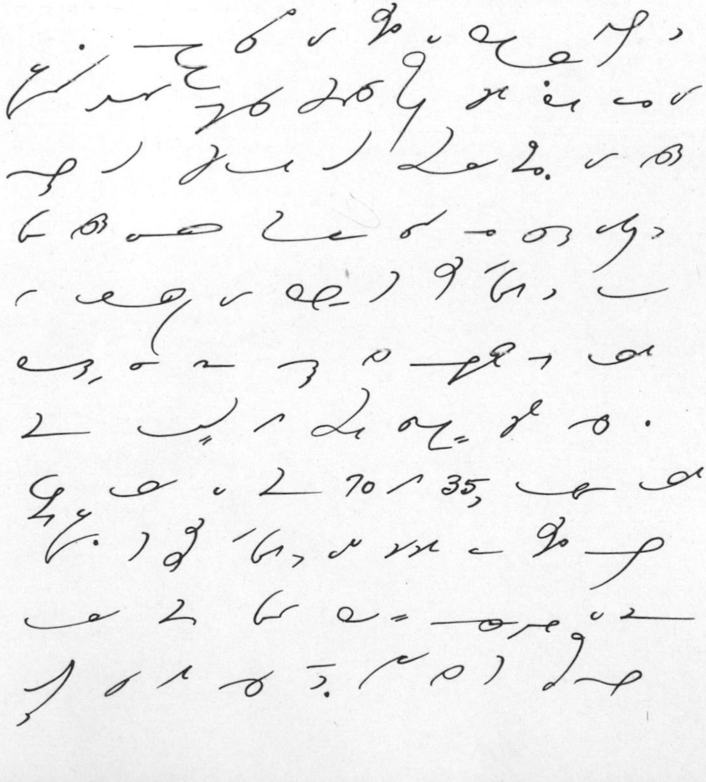

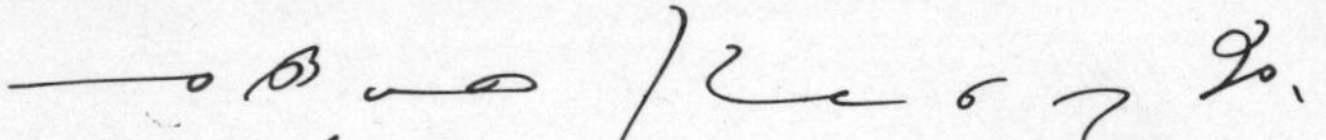

288.

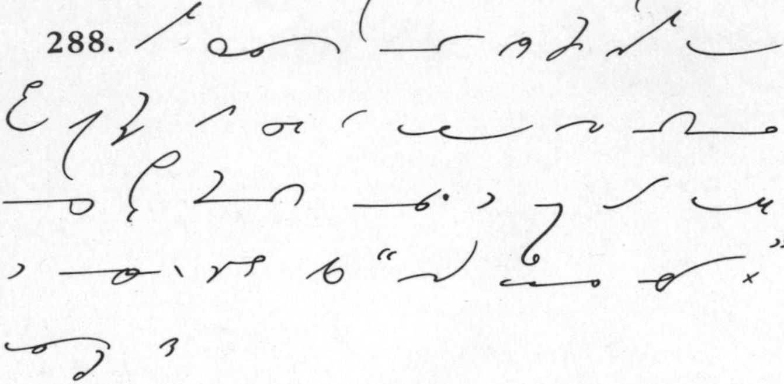

ASSIGNMENT 57

289. Drill on Previous Assignments

290. -sure is expressed by sh ish

291. -ward, -hood

292. Trans-

293. Super-, supr- *by comma s r above the line*

294. -ure *by r joined*

295. -quire *by ki, joined*

Reading and Writing Exercise

296.

(shorthand outlines)

297.

(shorthand outlines)

298. FOLLOW OUT A PLAN

(shorthand outlines)

(shorthand outlines)

299. An Artist

(shorthand outlines)

300.

(shorthand outlines)

301.

ASSIGNMENT 58

302. Drill on Previous Assignments

[shorthand outlines]

303. -ograph is expressed by the o hook placed up right.

[shorthand outlines]

304. -ical, -icle -acle: are expressed by disjoined k.

[shorthand outlines]

305. -sult *is expressed by backward*

(shorthand outlines)

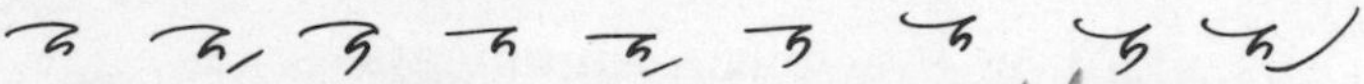

306. -gram, -grim *are expressed by g*

(shorthand outlines)

Reading and Writing Exercise

307. *(shorthand outlines)*

308. *(shorthand outlines)*

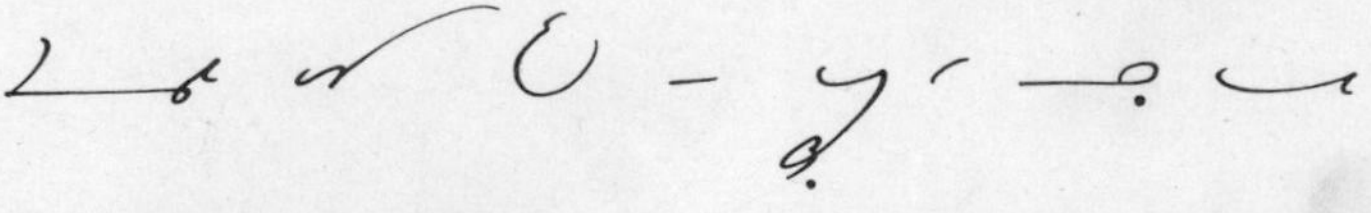

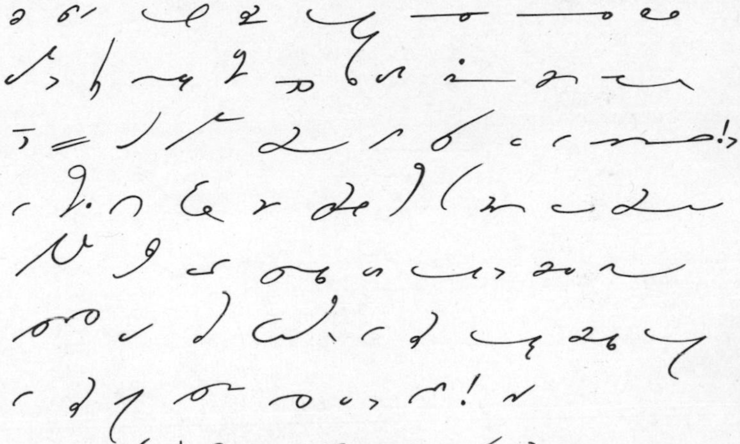

309.

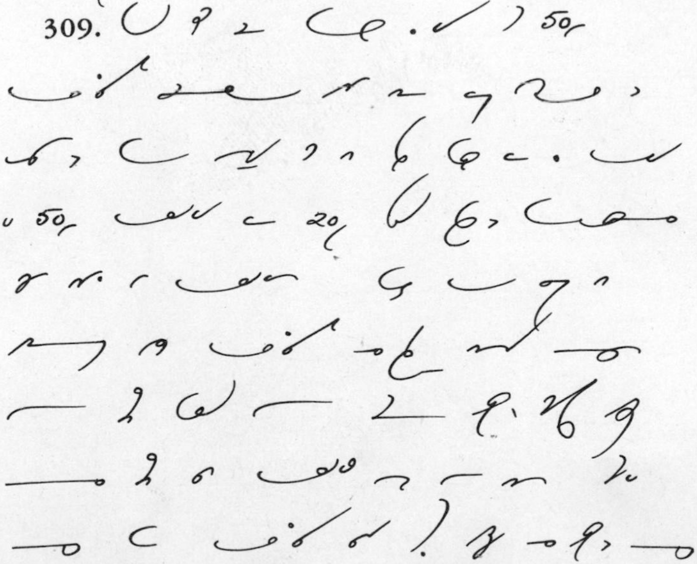

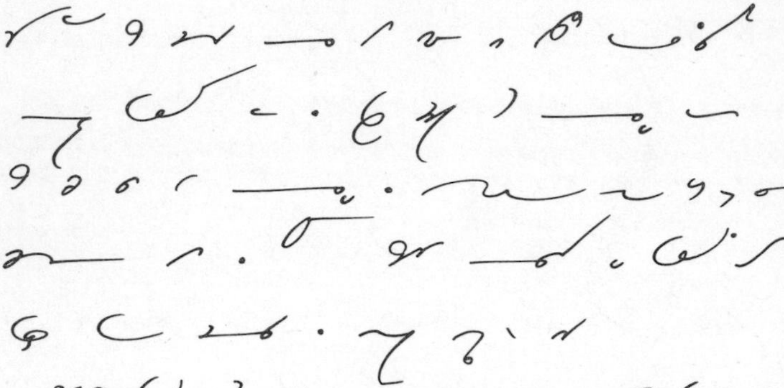

310.

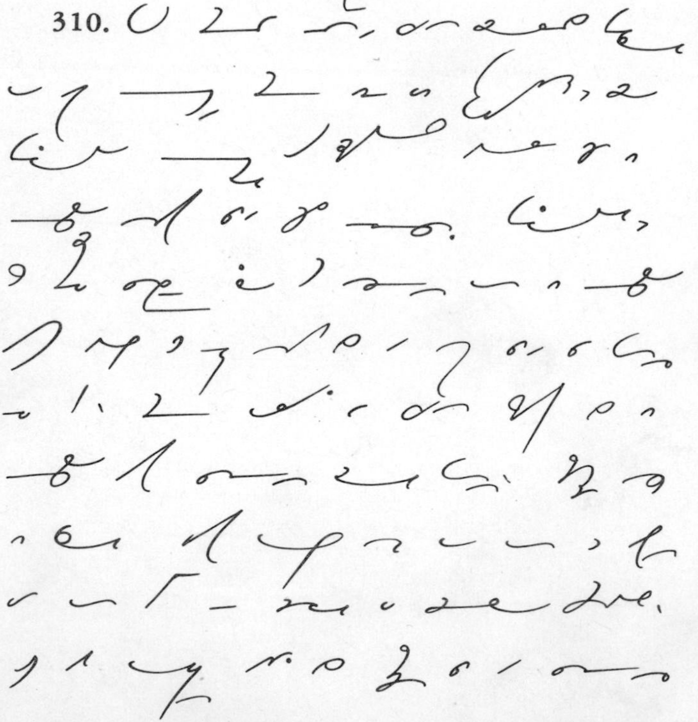

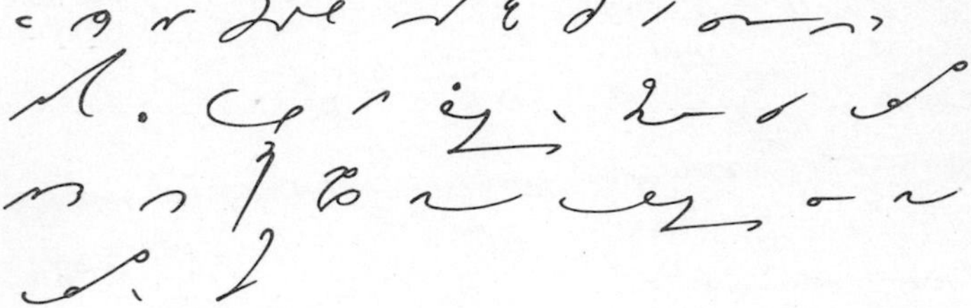

311.

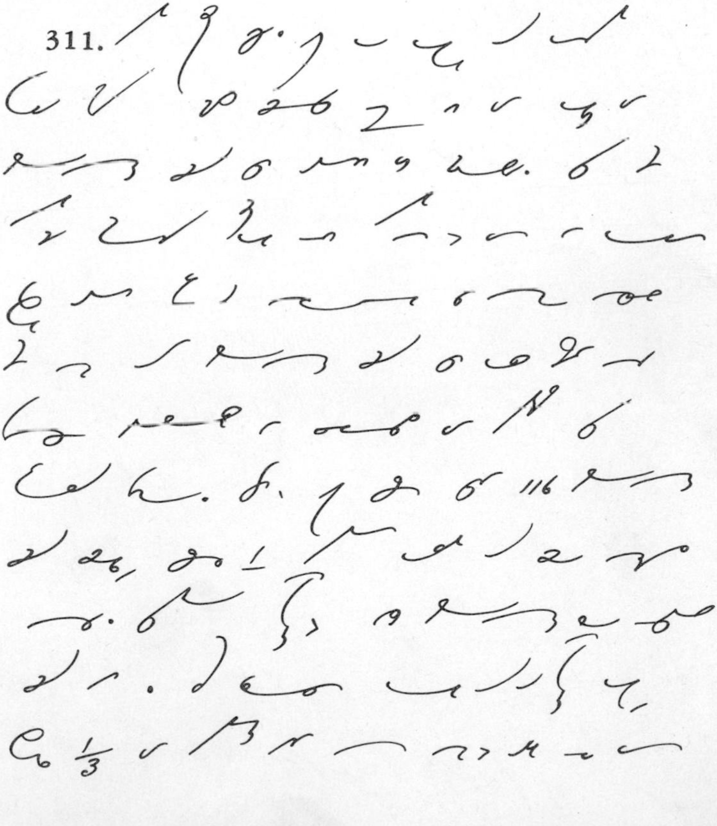

ASSIGNMENT 59

312. Drill on Previous Assignments *Thur.*

[shorthand outlines]

313. -spect - *expressed by sp*

[shorthand outlines]

314. Electr- *expressed by el*

[shorthand outlines]

315. -city, -sity *expressed* ,

[shorthand outlines]

expressed by

316. -ual *Joined l:-*

[shorthand outlines]

Reading and Writing Exercise

Read Tues.

317. [shorthand outlines]

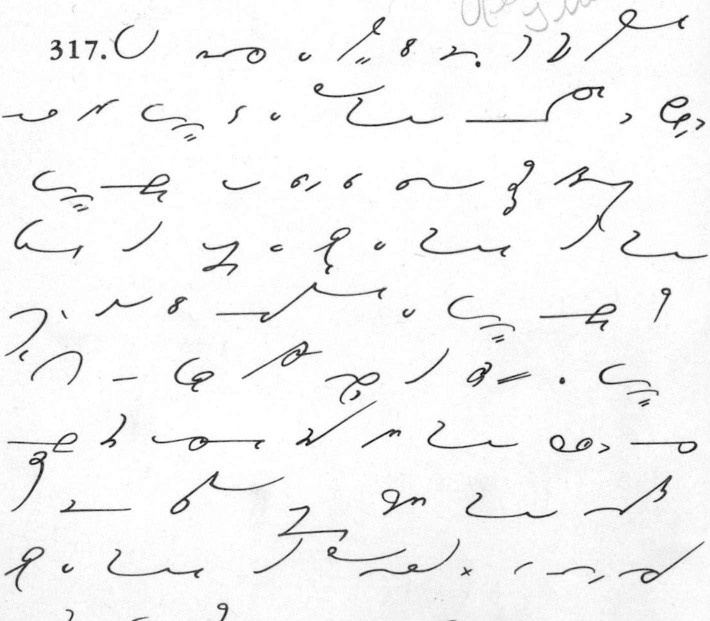

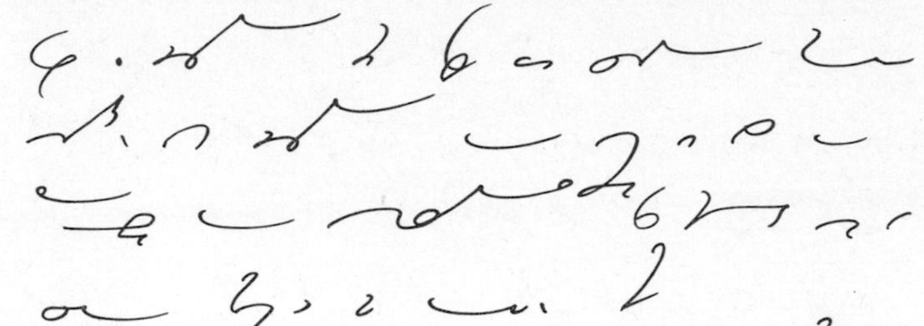

318.

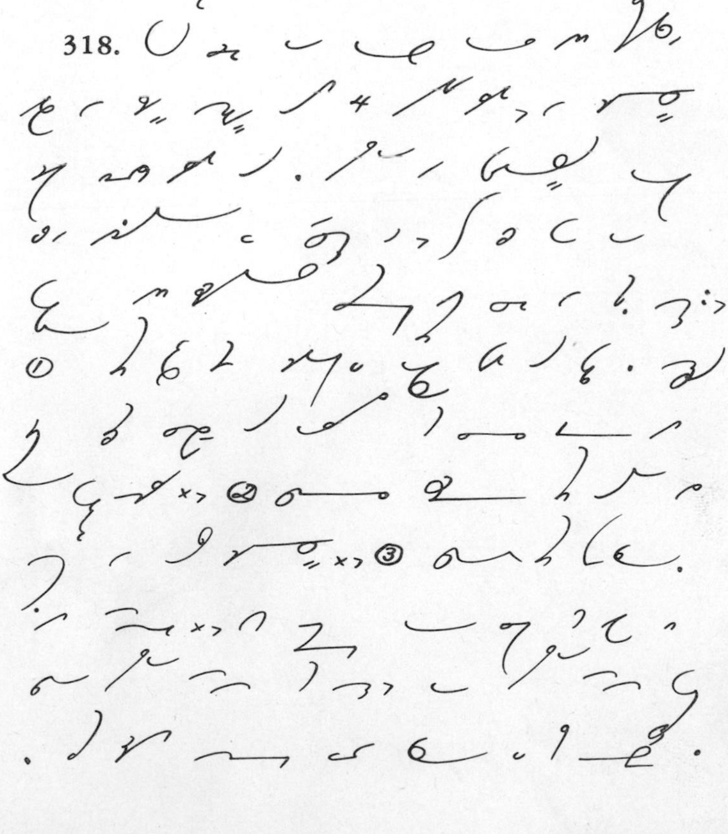

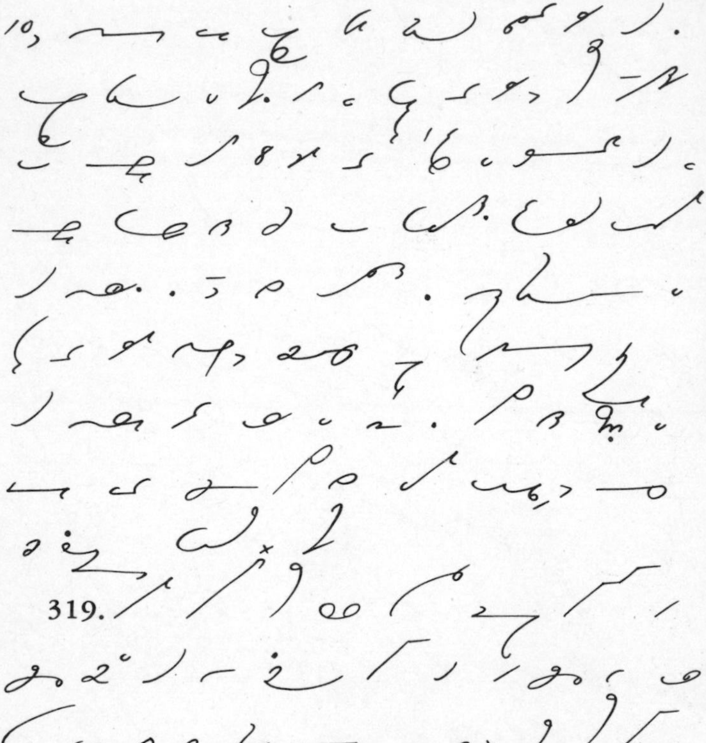

319.

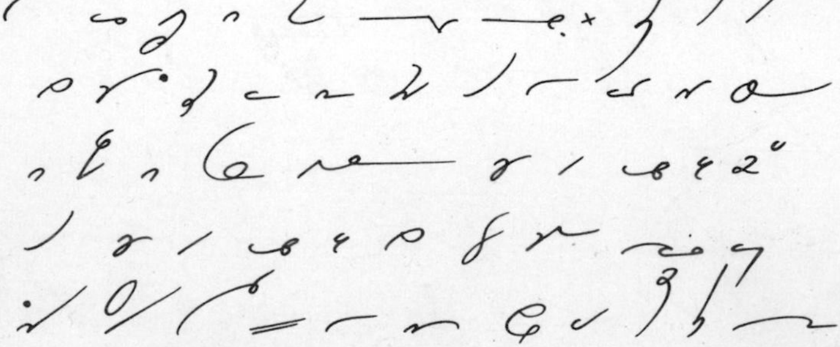

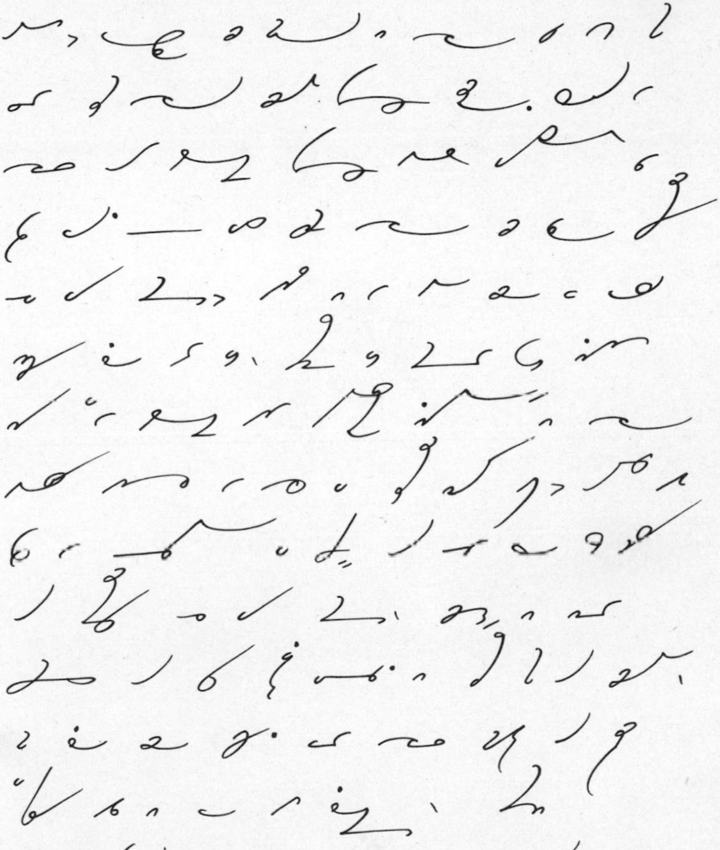

320.

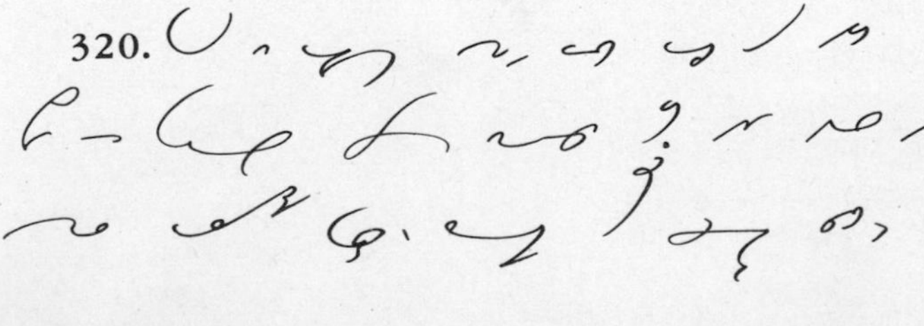

CHAPTER XI

ASSIGNMENT 60

321. Drill on Previous Assignments *3 lines*

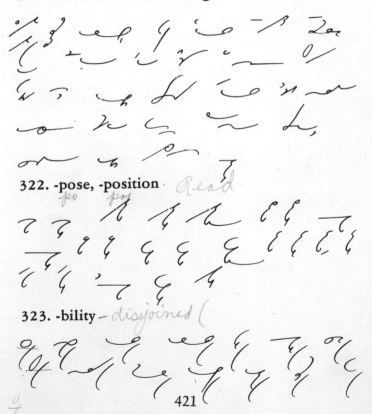

322. -pose, -position *Read*
po *pos*

323. -bility *- disjoined (*

324. -nity *blend*

325. -lity *by l*

326. -stic *by st*

Reading and Writing Exercise

327.

[shorthand outlines]

328. Do Enclosures Really Pay?

[shorthand outlines]

(shorthand outline content)

329.

(shorthand outline content)

ASSIGNMENT 61

330. Drill on Previous Assignments

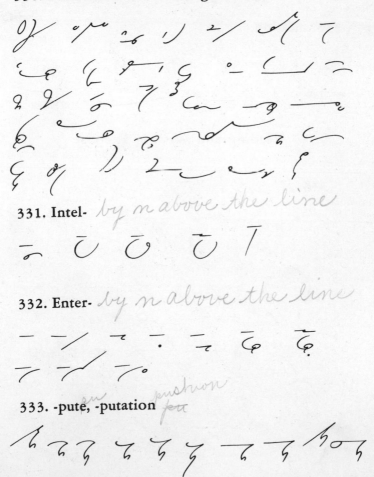

331. Intel- *by n above the line*

332. Enter- *by n above the line*

333. -pute, -putation

334. -cient

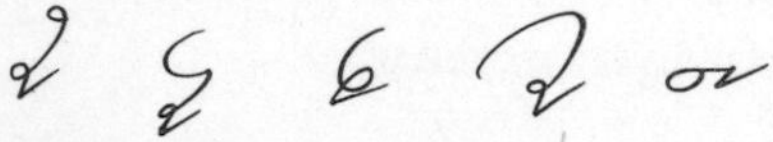

335. -fication

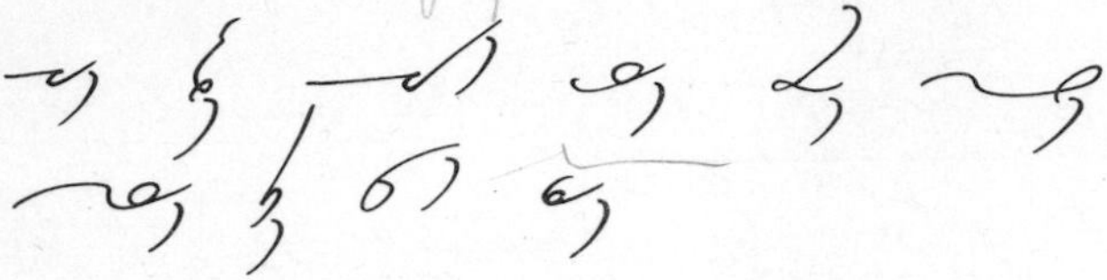

Reading and Writing Exercise

336.

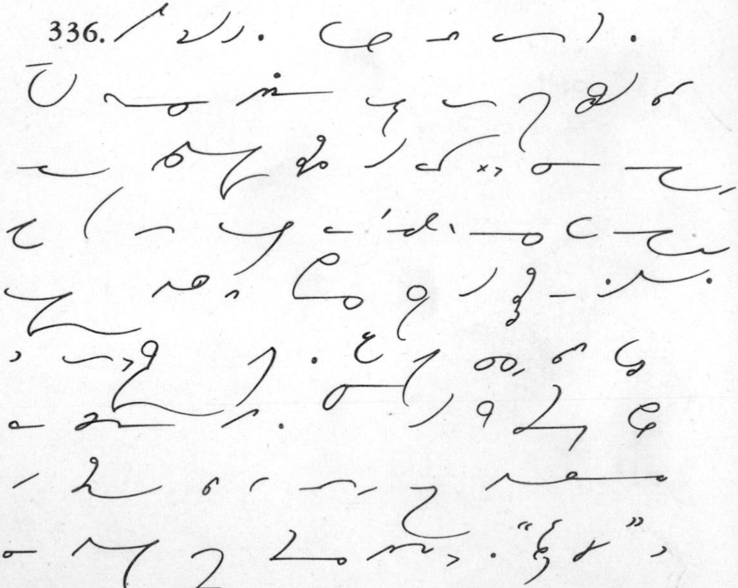

337.

338. The Postal Service

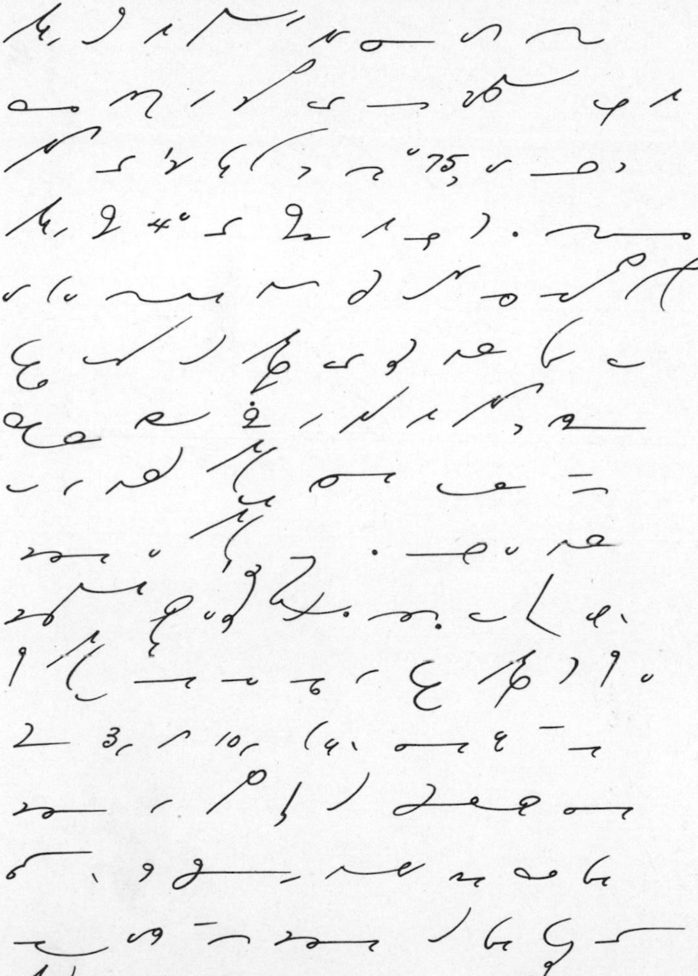

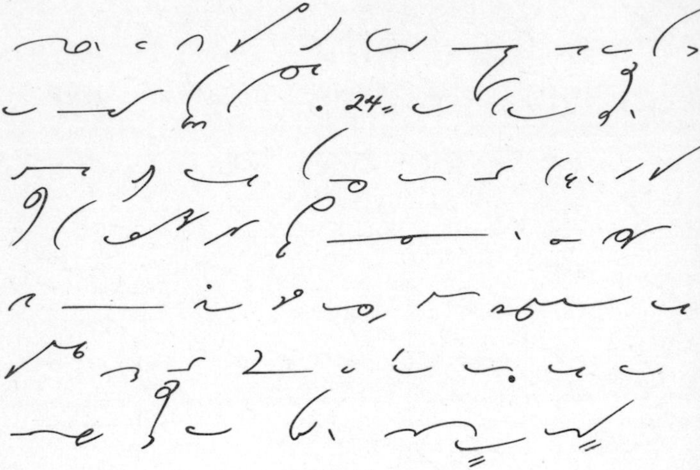

ASSIGNMENT 62

339. Drill on Previous Assignments

[shorthand outlines]

340. Detr- *by d above*

[shorthand outlines]

341. -scribe, -scription *scr - scru shion*

[shorthand outlines]

342. -pire *by pr joined*

[shorthand outlines]

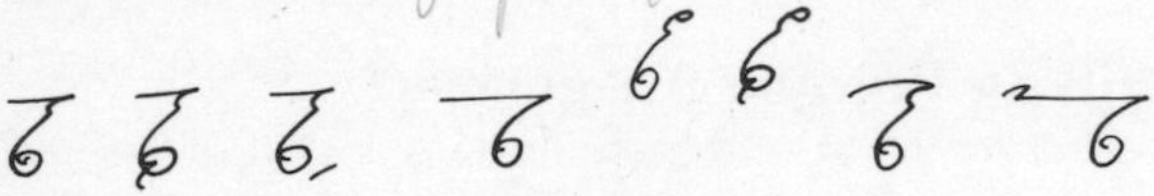

Reading and Writing Exercise

343. [shorthand outlines]

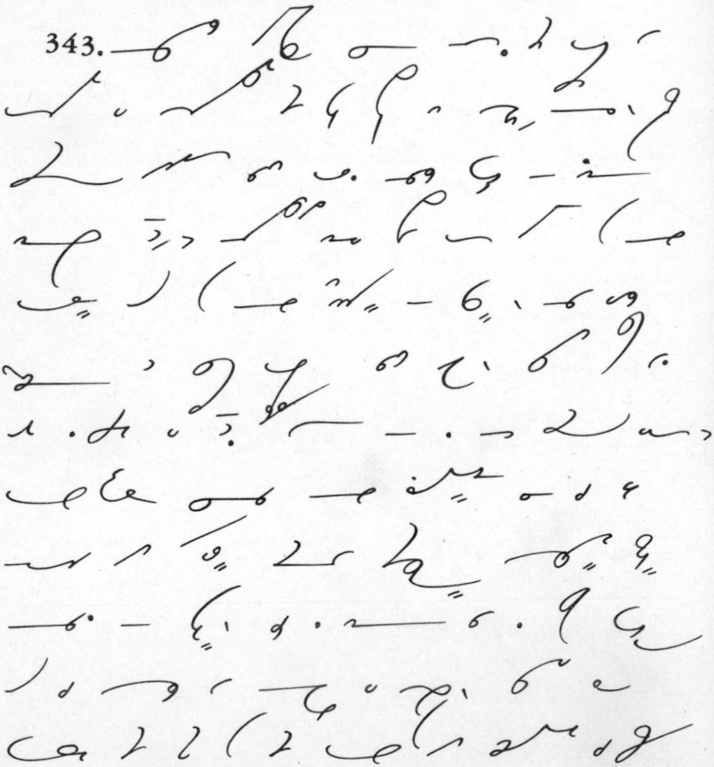

344.

(shorthand outlines)

345. (shorthand outlines)

346. Drill on Previous Assignments

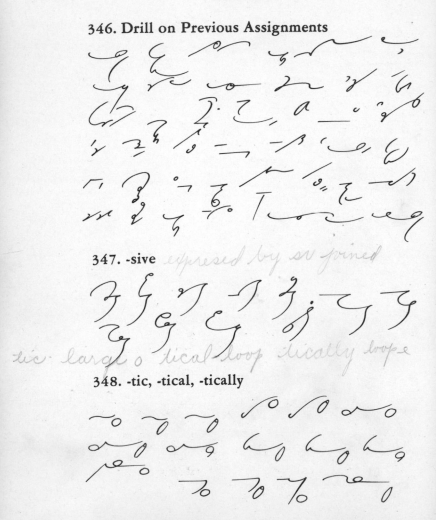

347. -sive *expressed by sv joined*

tic large o tical loop tically loope

348. -tic, -tical, -tically

349. Multi- expressed by mu.

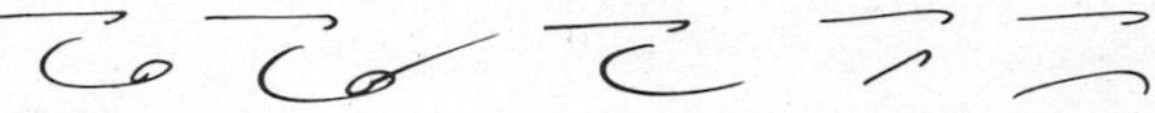

350. -ulate expressed by disjoined upper hook in the ing position

Reading and Writing Exercise

351.

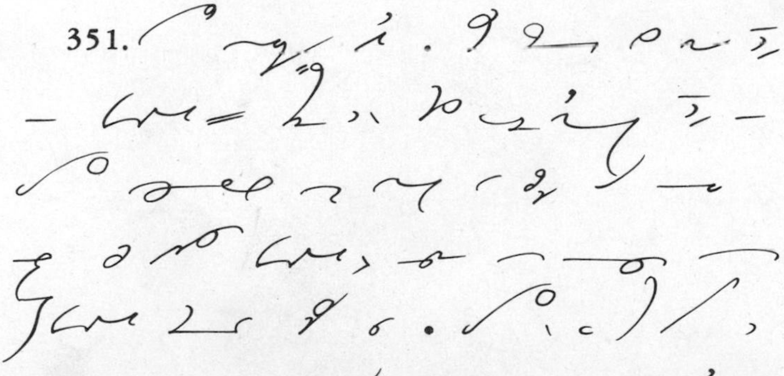

(shorthand outlines)

352.

(shorthand outlines)

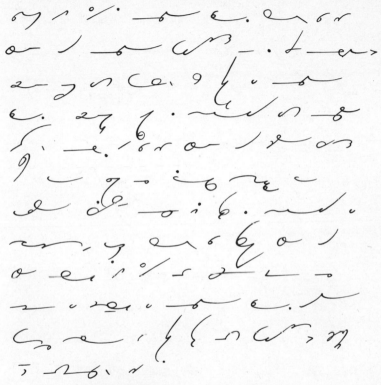

353. Membership in the House

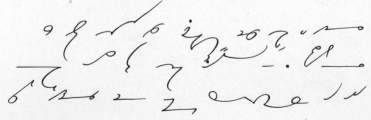

269, 278

ASSIGNMENT 64

354. Drill on Previous Assignments

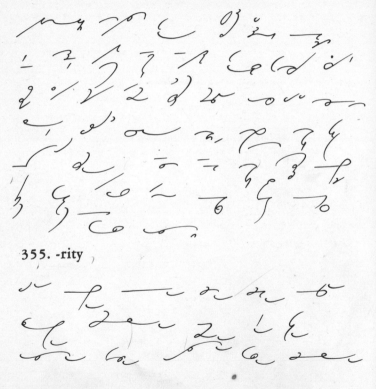

355. -rity

356. -jure

357. Constr-

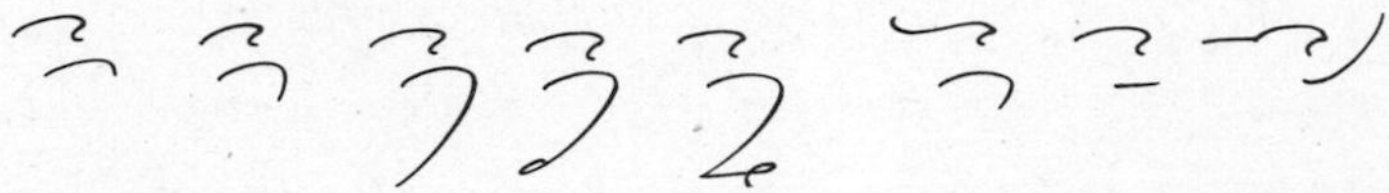

358. Instr-

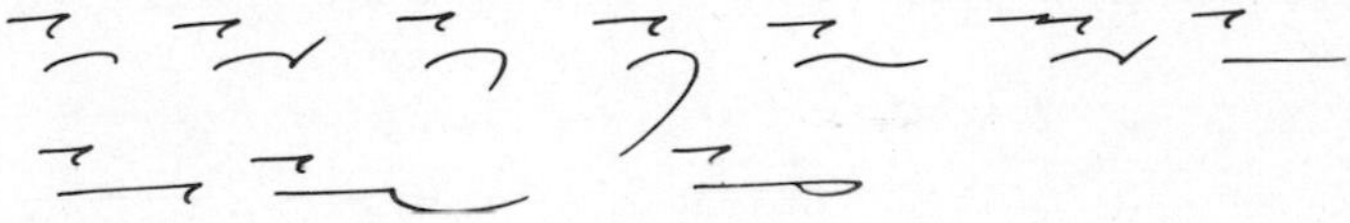

Reading and Writing Exercise

359.

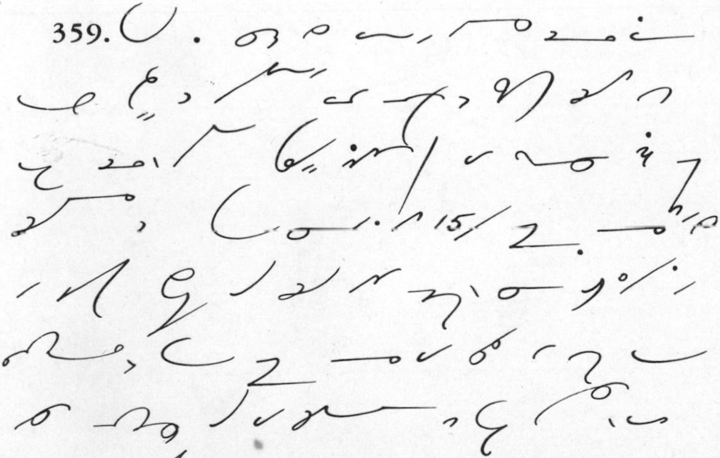

360.

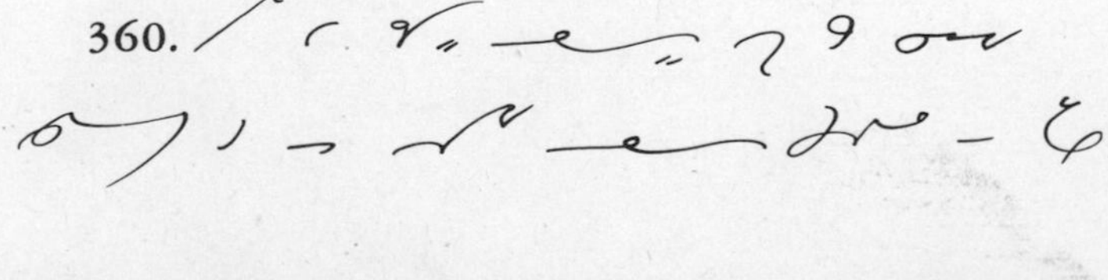

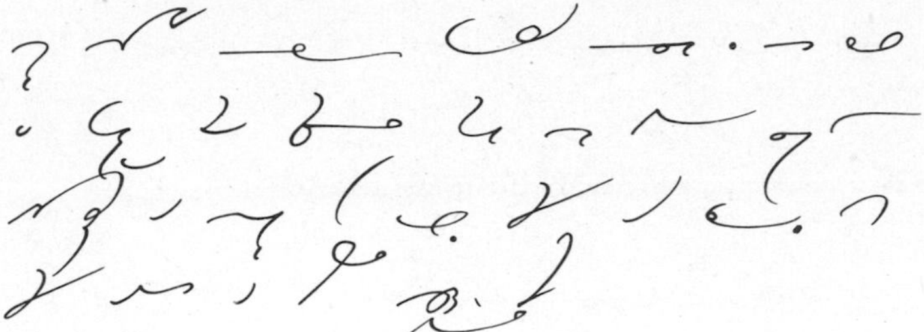

361.

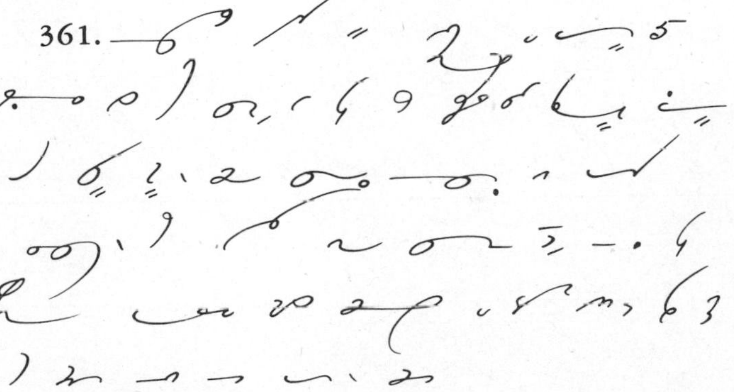

362.

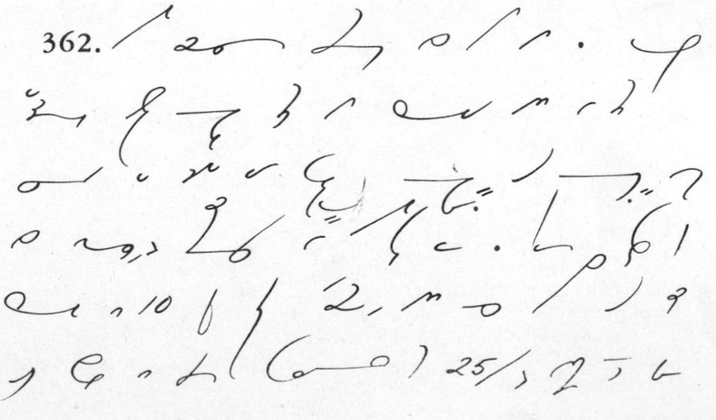

(shorthand outlines)

363. BUSINESS STATIONERY

(shorthand outlines)

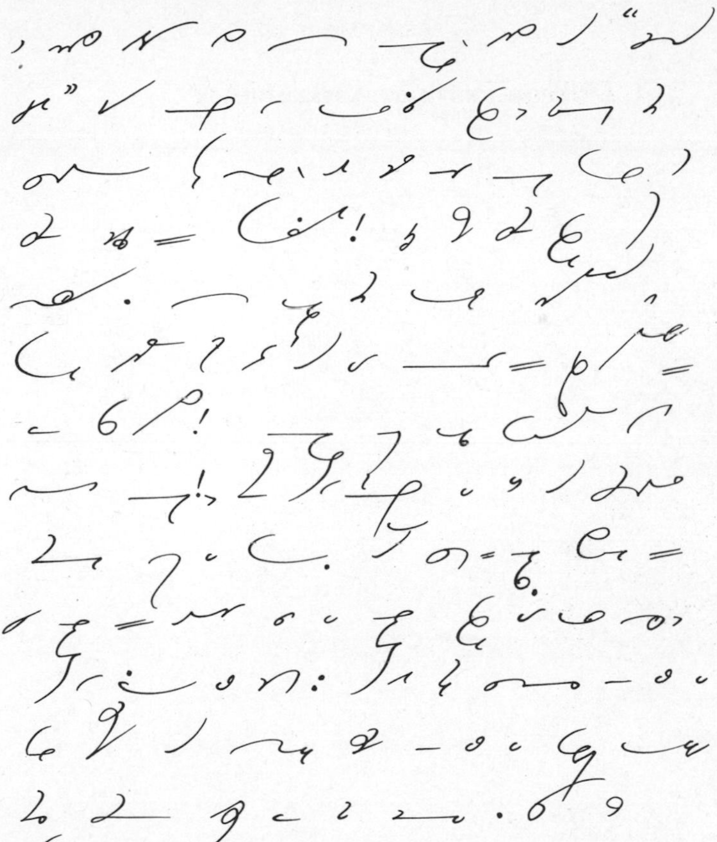

364. Drill on Previous Assignments

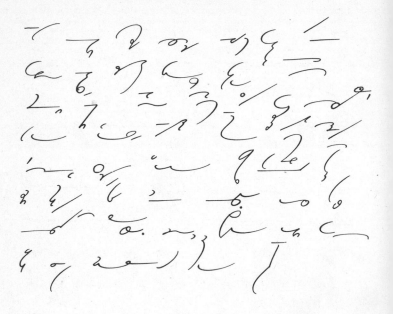

365. Self-

366. -nment

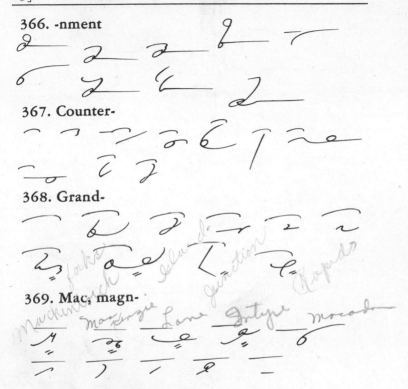

367. Counter-

368. Grand-

369. Mac; magn-

Reading and Writing Exercise

370.

371.

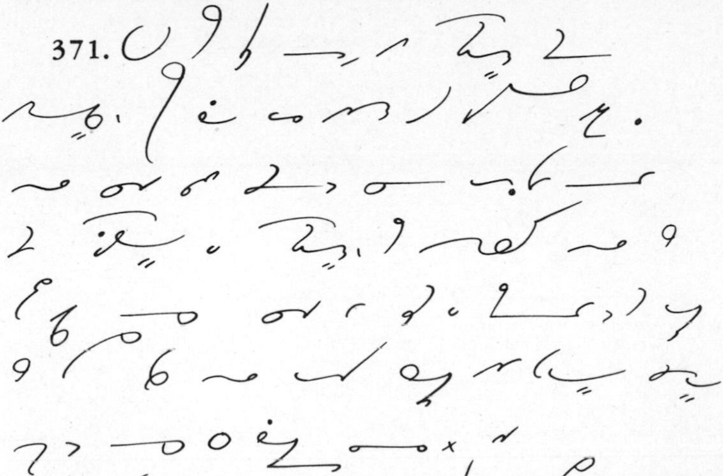

372.

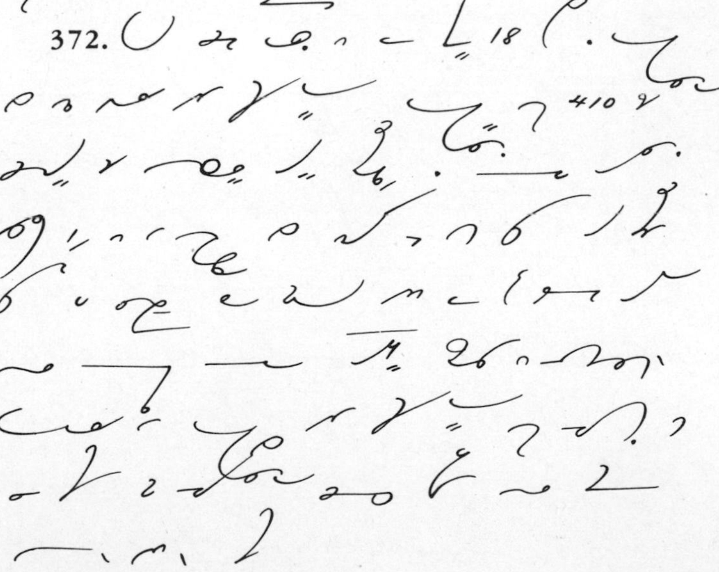

373. Self-control

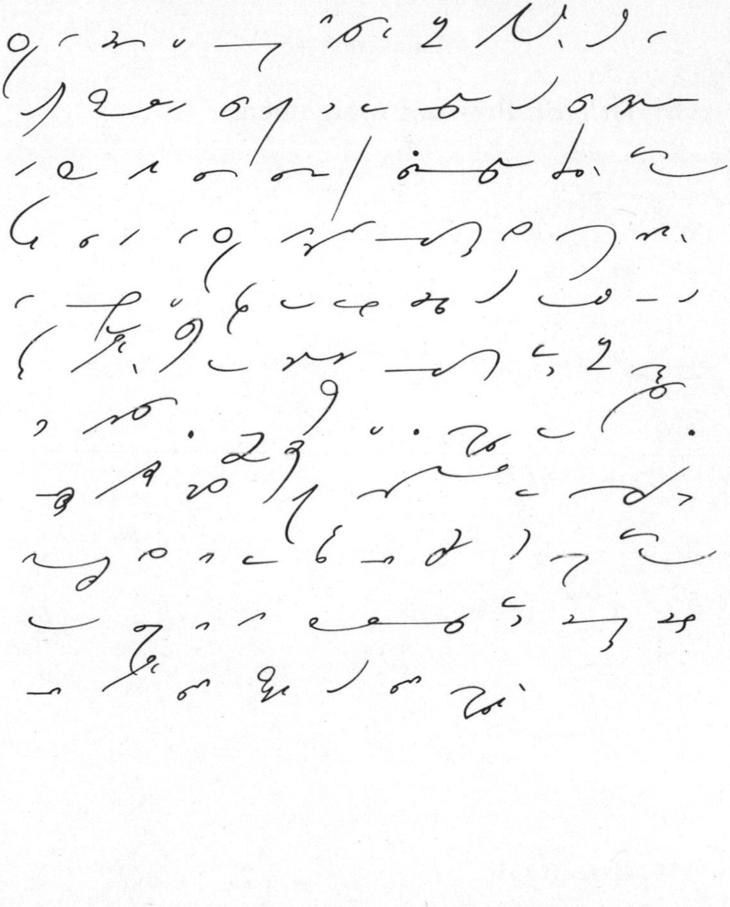

374. Drill on Previous Assignments

375. Extr-, excl-

376. Decl-

377. -mental

378. logy, -logical

Reading and Writing Exercise

379.

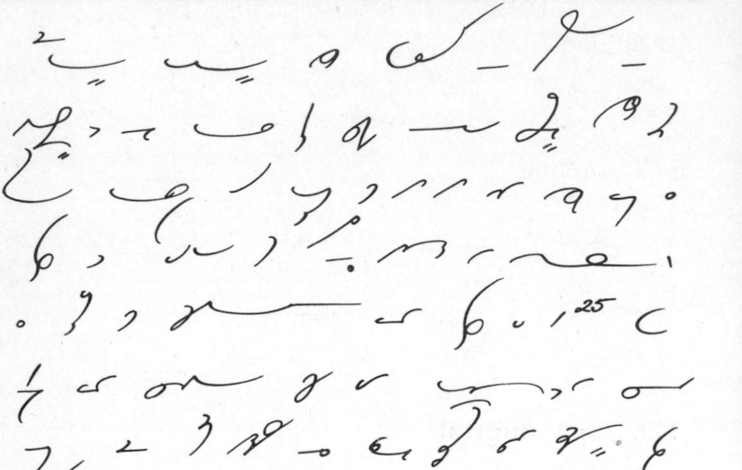

380.

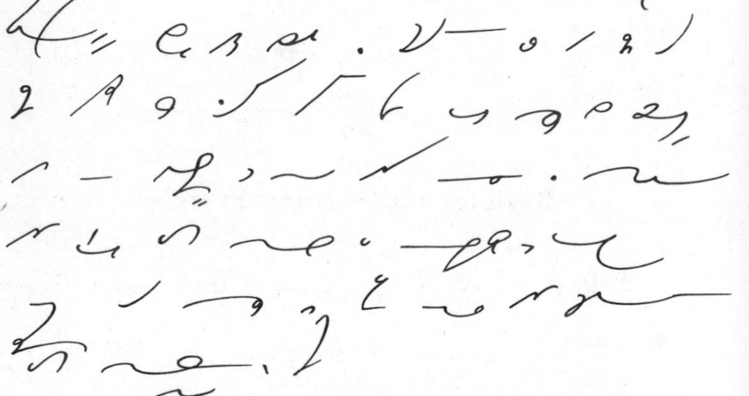

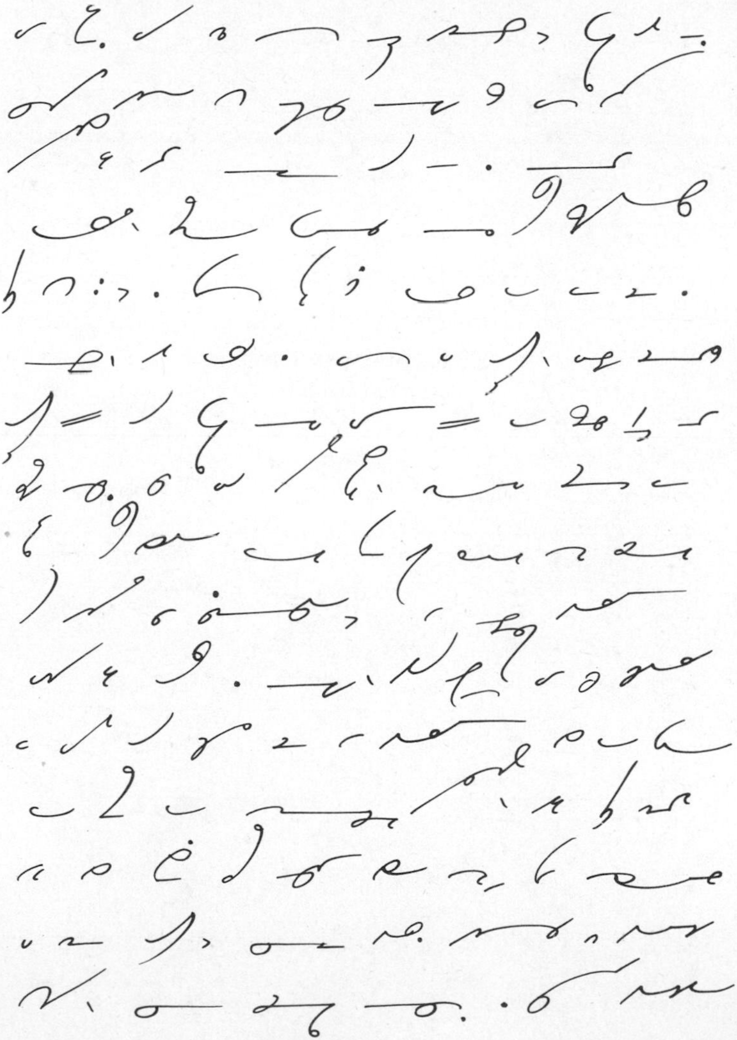

(shorthand outlines)

381. Business Dress

(shorthand outlines)

382. Drill on Previous Assignments

383. -flect, -flict

384. -mity

385. -gency

386. Susp-, suscep-

387. Circum-

Reading and Writing Exercise

388.

(shorthand outlines)

23 — — —

(shorthand outlines)

389. *(shorthand outlines)*

[shorthand outlines]

390. Playing the Game

[shorthand outlines]

[shorthand outlines]

391. Leadership

[shorthand outlines]

ASSIGNMENT 68

392. Drill on Previous Assignments

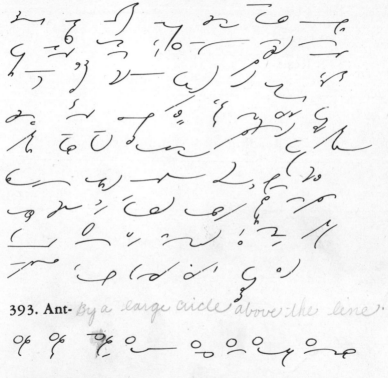

393. Ant- *By a large circle above the line.*

394. -egraph

395. Recl-

396. Retr-

397. Restr-

Reading and Writing Exercise

398.

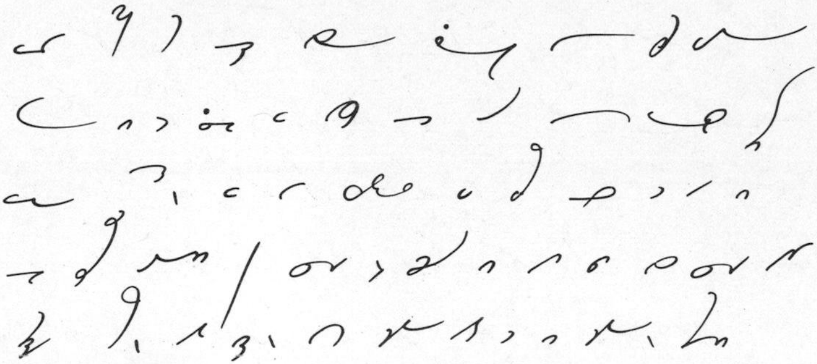

399.

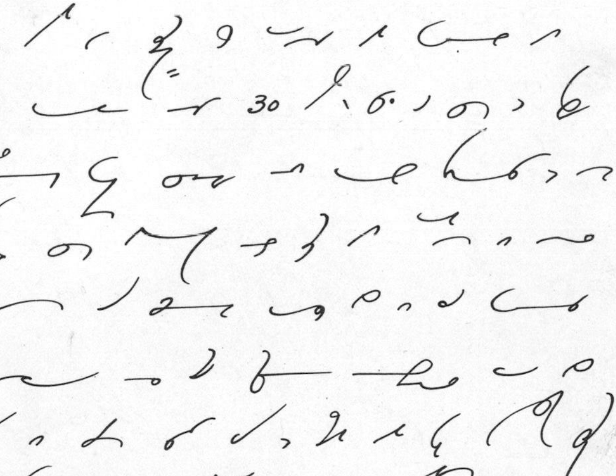

400.

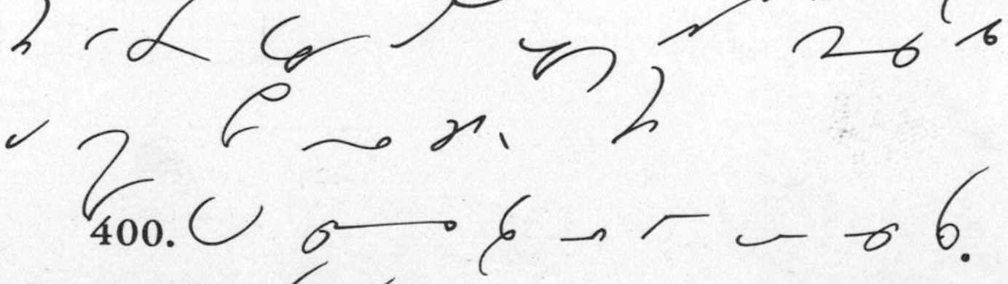

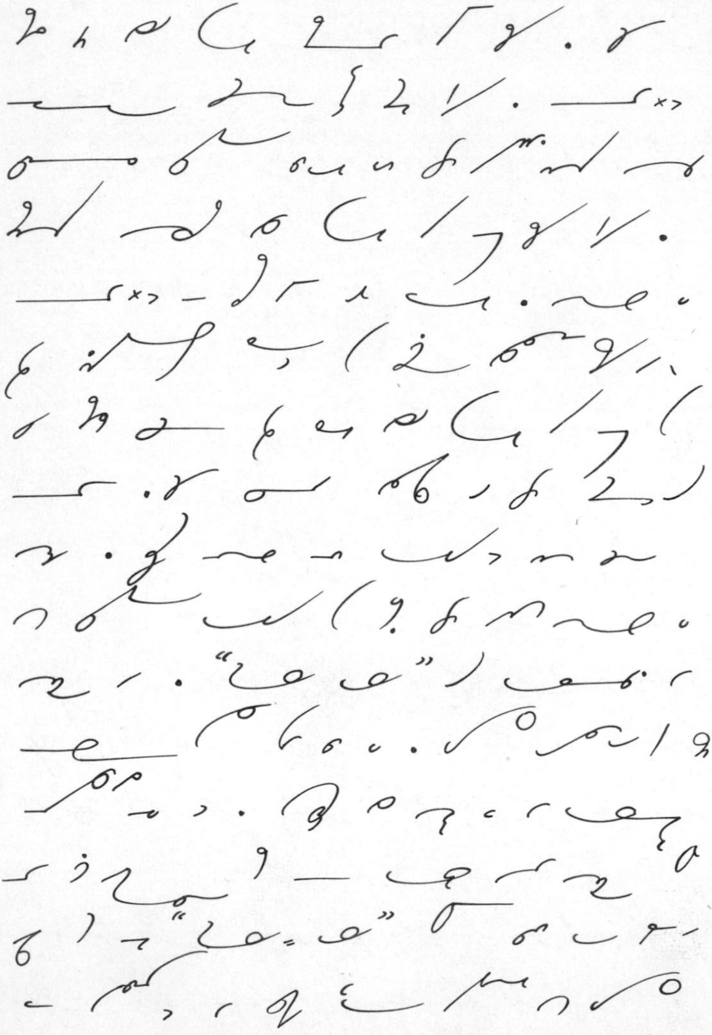

401.

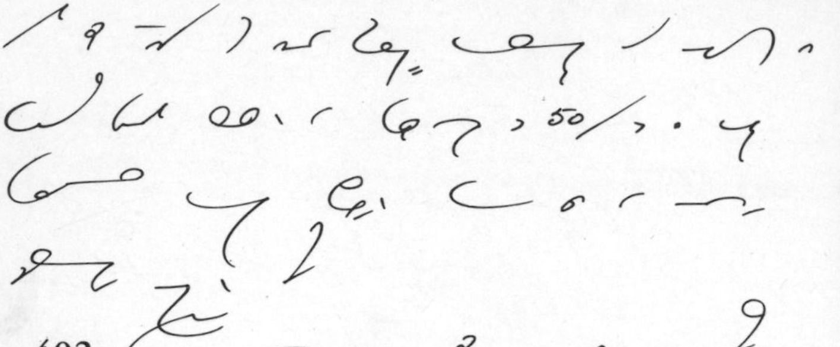

402.

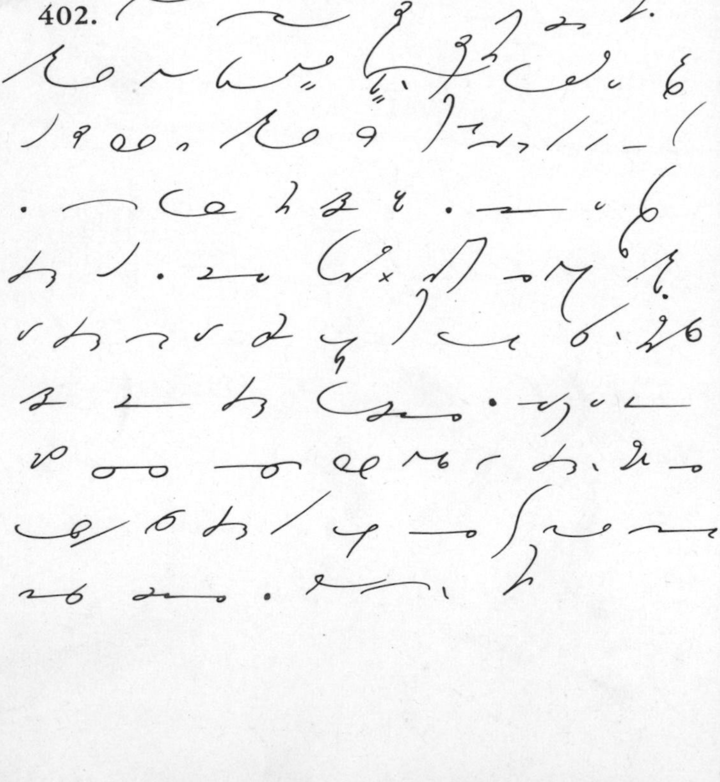

CHAPTER XII

403. Drill on Previous Assignments

[shorthand outlines]

404. States and Territories. The abbreviations used in the following list are those adopted by the Post Office Department:

Ala.	*(outline)*	Conn.	*(outline)*	Hawaii	*(outline)*
Alaska	*(outline)*	Del.	*(outline)*	Idaho	*(outline)*
Ariz.	*(outline)*	D. C.	*(outline)*	Ill.	*(outline)*
Ark.	*(outline)*	Fla.	*(outline)*	Ind.	*(outline)*
Calif.	*(outline)*	Ga.	*(outline)*	Iowa	*(outline)*
Colo.	*(outline)*	Guam	*(outline)*	Kans.	*(outline)*

Ky.		N. H.		R. I.	
La.		N. J.		S. C.	
Maine		N. Mex.		S. Dak.	
Md.		N. Y.		Tenn.	
Mass.		N. C.		Tex.	
Mich.		N. Dak.		Utah	
Minn.		Ohio		Vt.	
Miss.		Okla.		Va.	
Mo.		Oreg.		Wash.	
Mont.		Pa.	6	W. Va.	
Nebr.		P. I.		Wis.	
Nev.		P. R.		Wyo.	

405. Principal Cities of the United States.   The following names of cities are arranged in the order of their population:

New York	New Orleans	New Haven
Chicago	Cincinnati	Fort Worth
Philadelphia	Kansas City	Miami
Los Angeles	Seattle	Des Moines
Detroit	Indianapolis	Salt Lake City
Cleveland	St. Paul	Yonkers
St. Louis	Jersey City	Albany
Baltimore	Rochester	San Diego
Boston	Toledo	New Bedford
Pittsburgh	Columbus	Lowell
San Francisco	Denver	Reading
Buffalo	Atlanta	Duluth
Washington	Omaha	Elizabeth
Milwaukee	San Antonio	Canton
Newark	Syracuse	El Paso
Minneapolis	Richmond	Spokane

Reading and Writing Exercise

406.

(shorthand outlines)

407. SHORTHAND

(shorthand outlines)

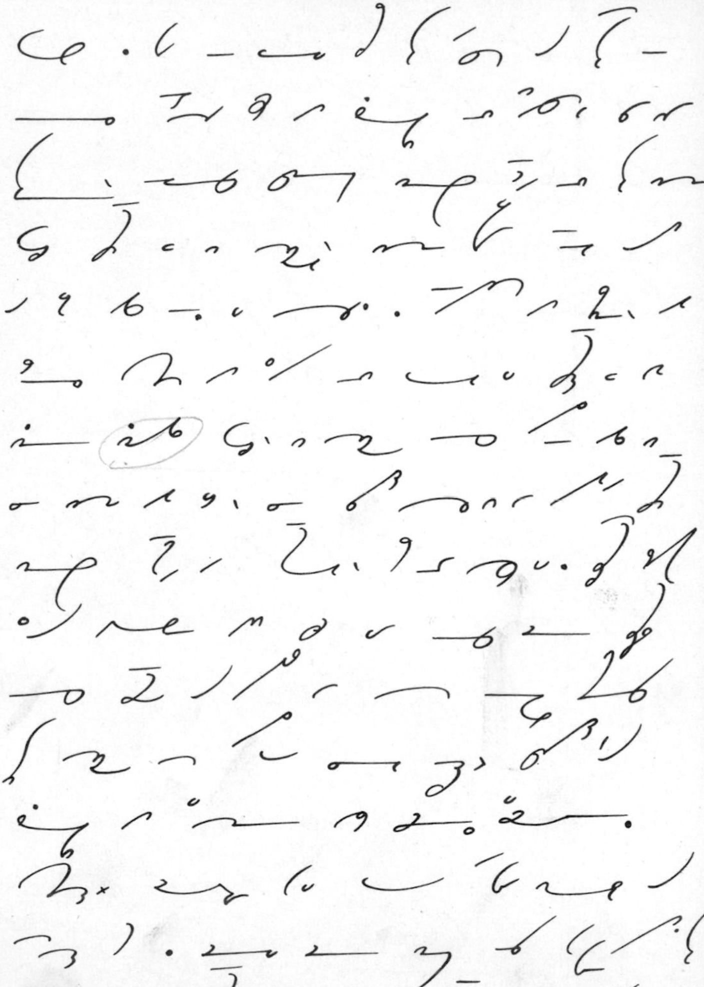

408. Drill on Previous Assignments.

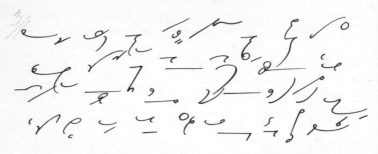

409. The terminations *burg, ville, field, port* may generally be expressed by the first letter, joined or disjoined as convenient; *ford,* by *fd; ington,* by a disjoined *tn;* and *ingham,* by a disjoined *m:*

Harrisburg	Knoxville	Oxford
Petersburg	Pittsfield	Rockford
Fitchburg	Greenfield	Milford
Newburgh	Plainfield	Kensington
Danville	Davenport	Arlington
Zanesville	Newport	Birmingham
Evansville	Shreveport	Nottingham

NOTE: A distinction between *ton* and *town* is made as follows:

Johnston	Johnstown	Charleston	Charlestown

410. The names of cities and states often may be joined:

Buffalo, N. Y.		St. Louis, Mo.	
St. Paul, Minn.		Rochester, N. Y.	
Boston, Mass.		Baltimore, Md.	
Detroit, Mich.		Memphis, Tenn.	
Chicago, Ill.		Louisville, Ky.	
Denver, Colo.		Minneapolis, Minn.	
Omaha, Nebr.		Washington, D. C.	

Learn

411. When the words "State of" precede the name of a state, omit *of* and join the words, if convenient:

Write

State of N. Y.		State of Mass.	
State of Nebr.		State of Pa.	
State of Ill.		State of La.	
State of N. J.		State of Ga.	
State of Miss.		State of Minn.	

Reading and Writing Exercise

412.

413.

ASSIGNMENT 71

414. Phrase Drill

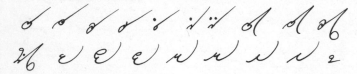

415. Brief-Form Drill

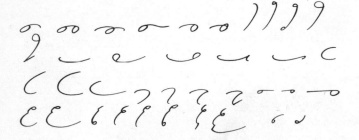

Reading and Writing Exercise

416.

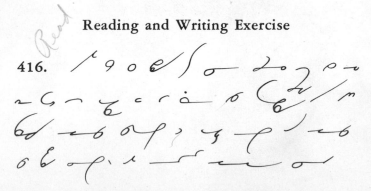

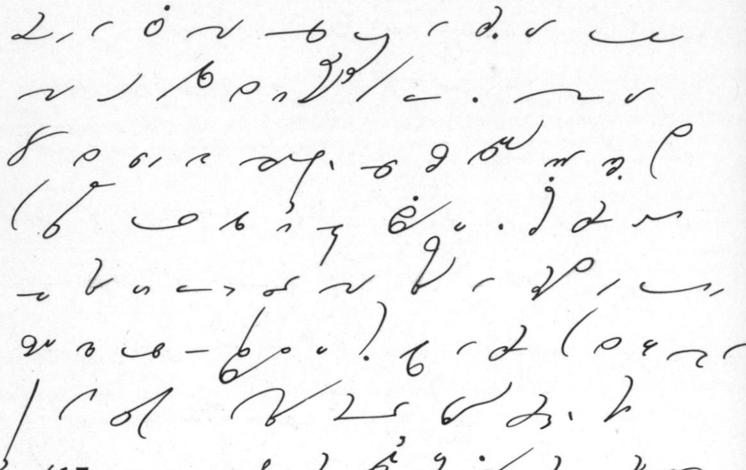

417.

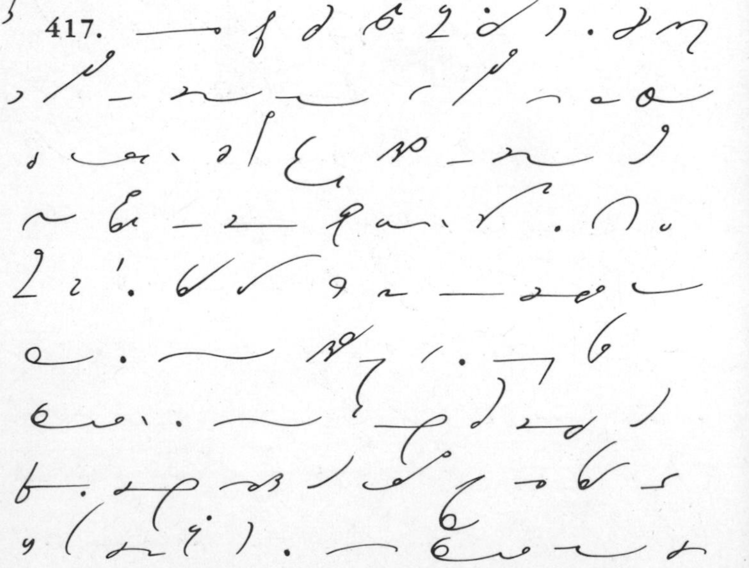

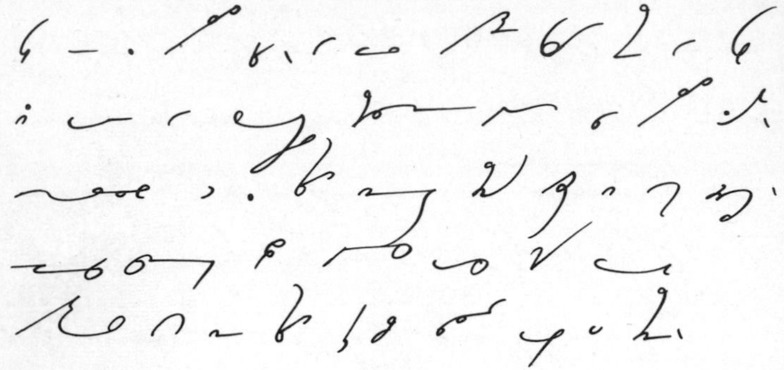

Assignment 72

418. Phrase Drill

419. Brief-Form Drill

Reading and Writing Exercise

420.

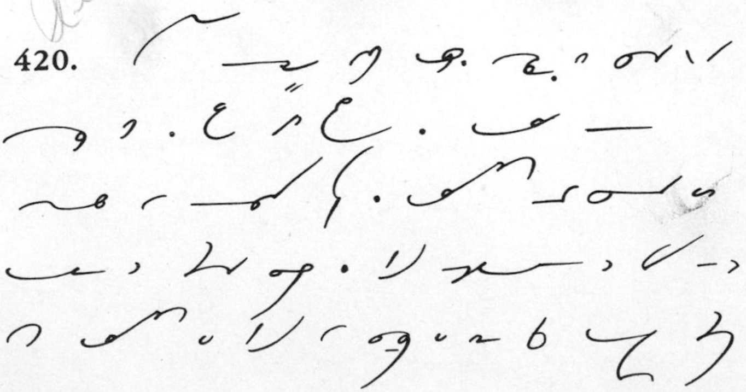

421.

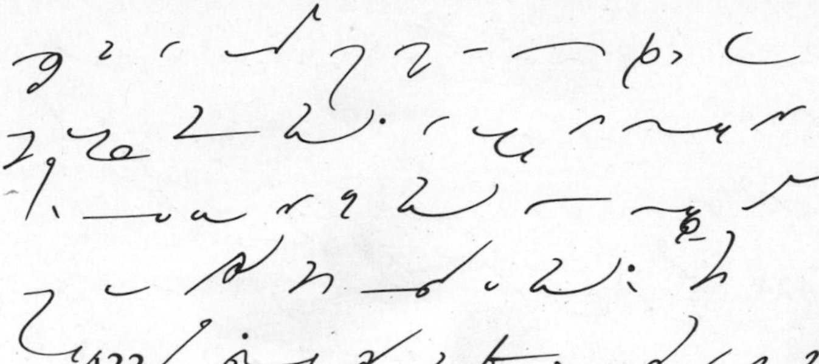

422.

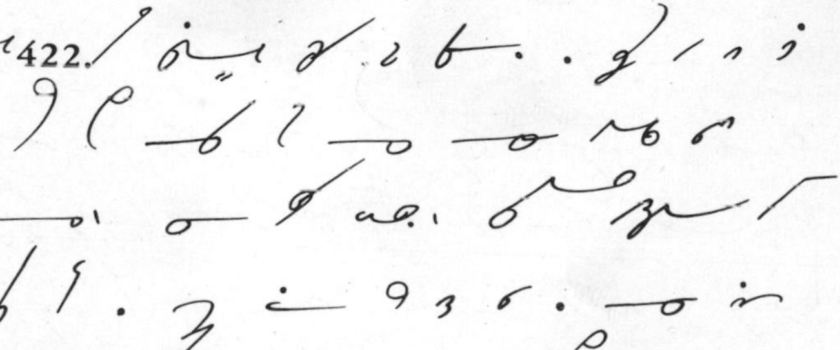

423.

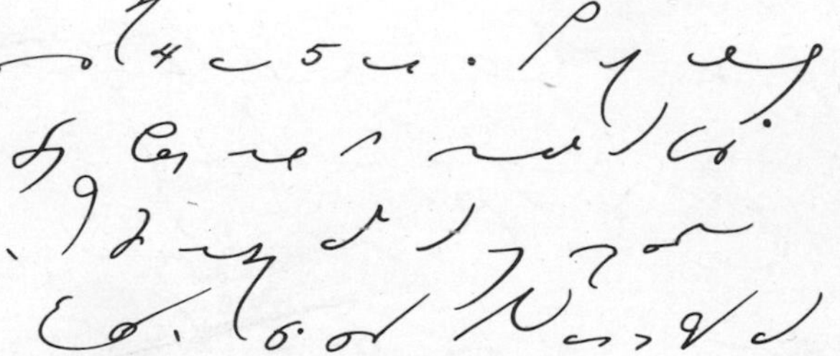

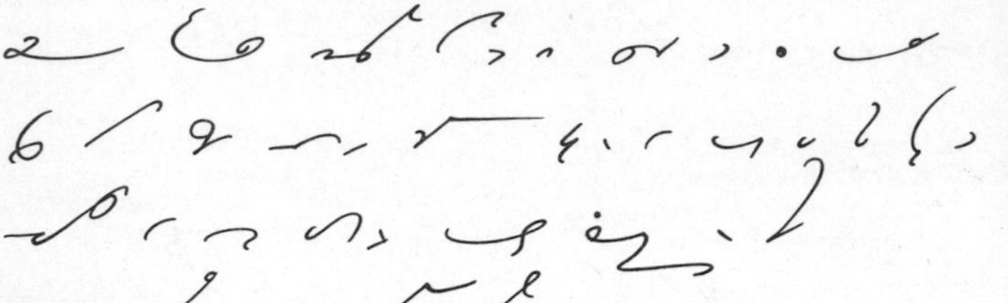

424.

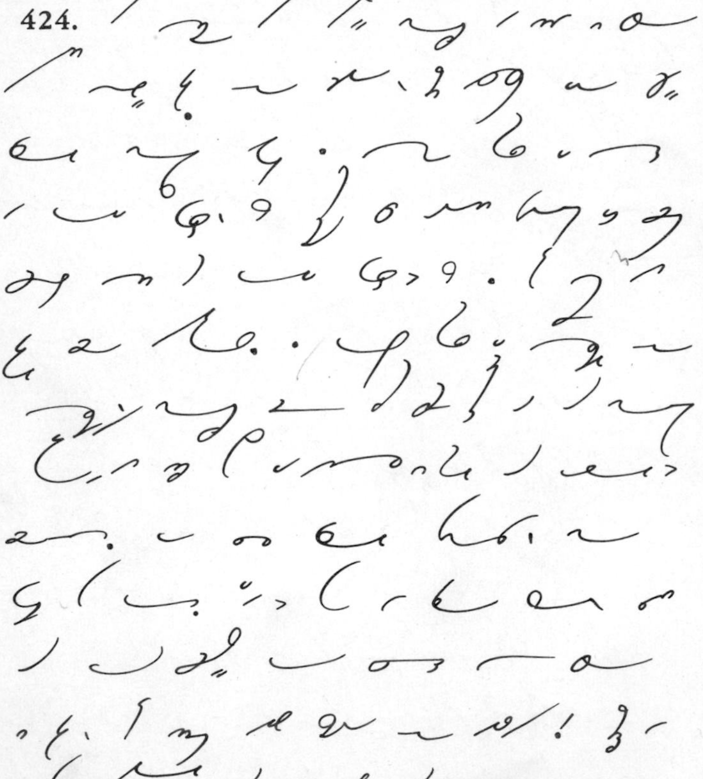

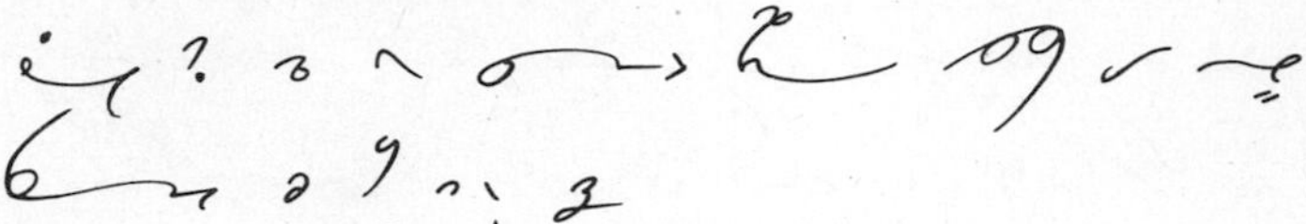

425.

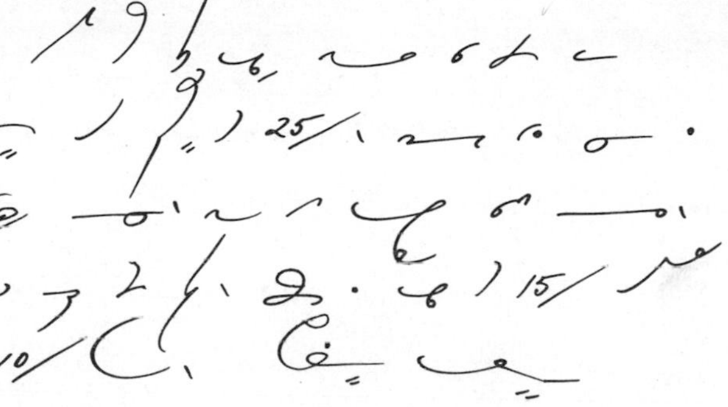

426. Nine Lessons in Living

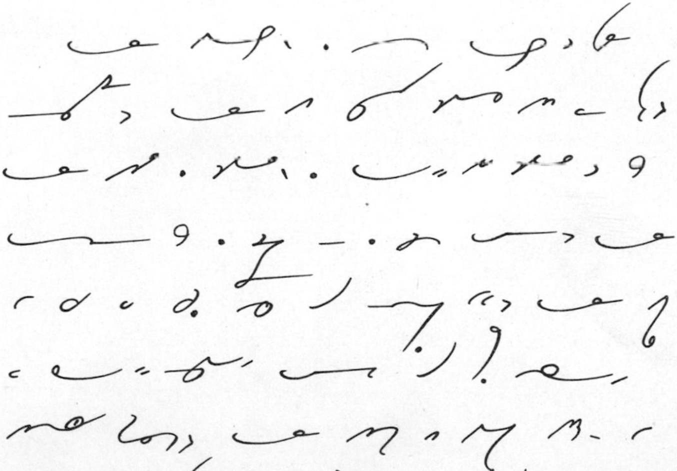

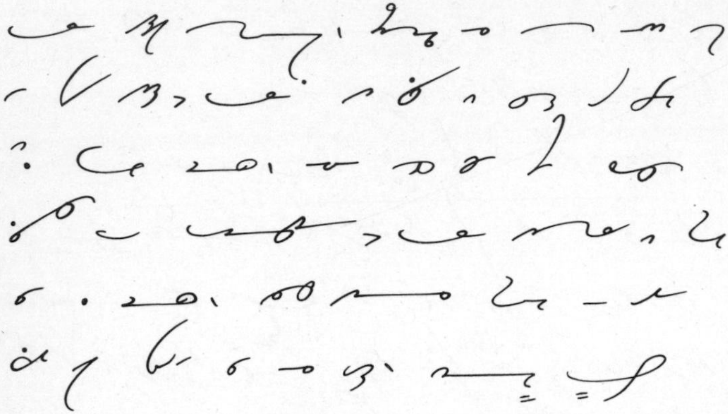

ASSIGNMENT 73

427. Phrase Drill

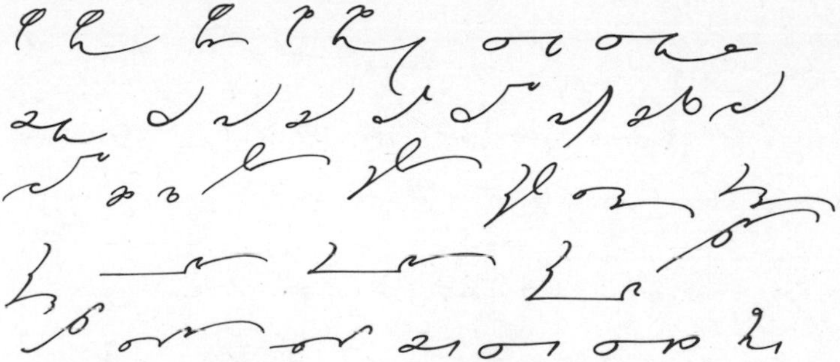

428. Brief-Form Drill

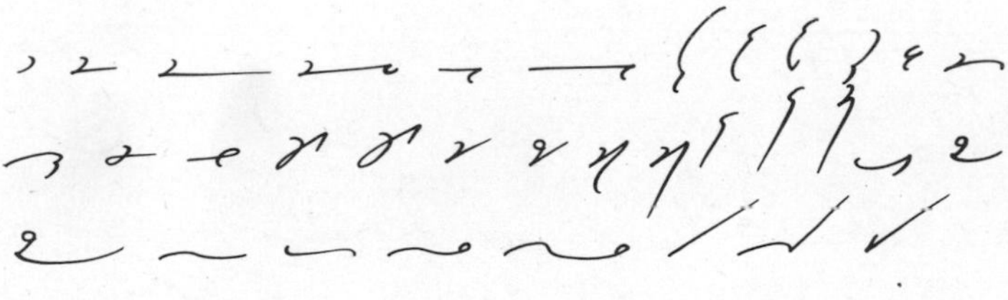

Reading and Writing Exercise

429. 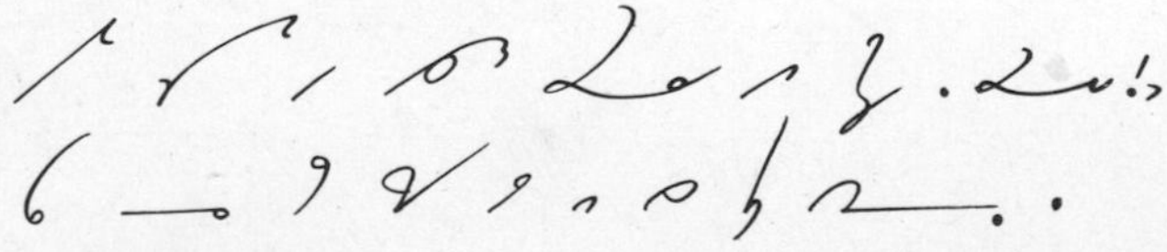

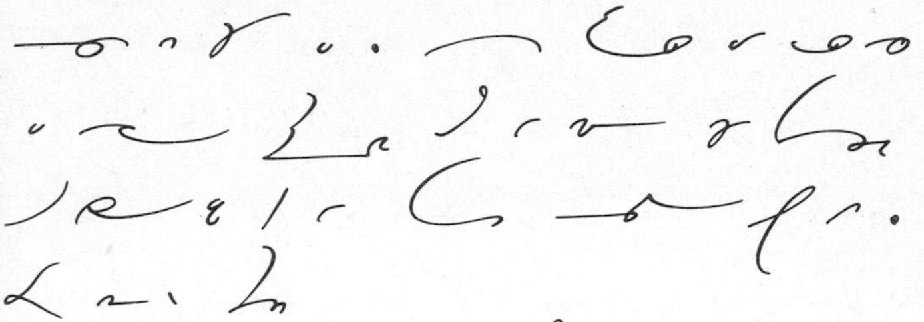

430. 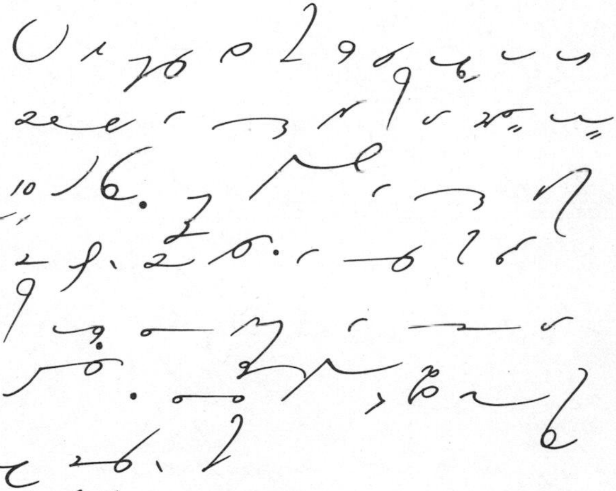

431. 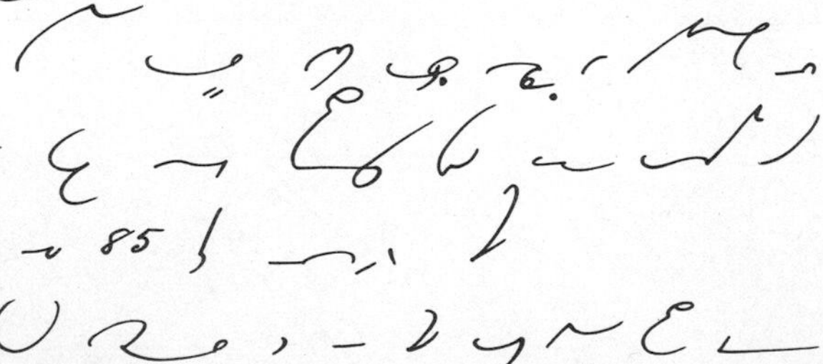

432. 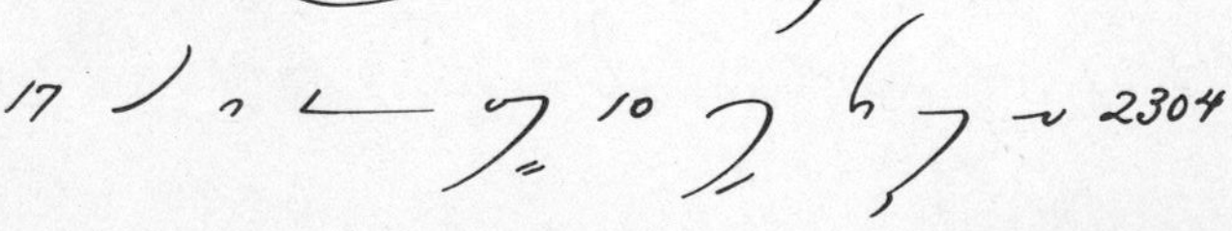

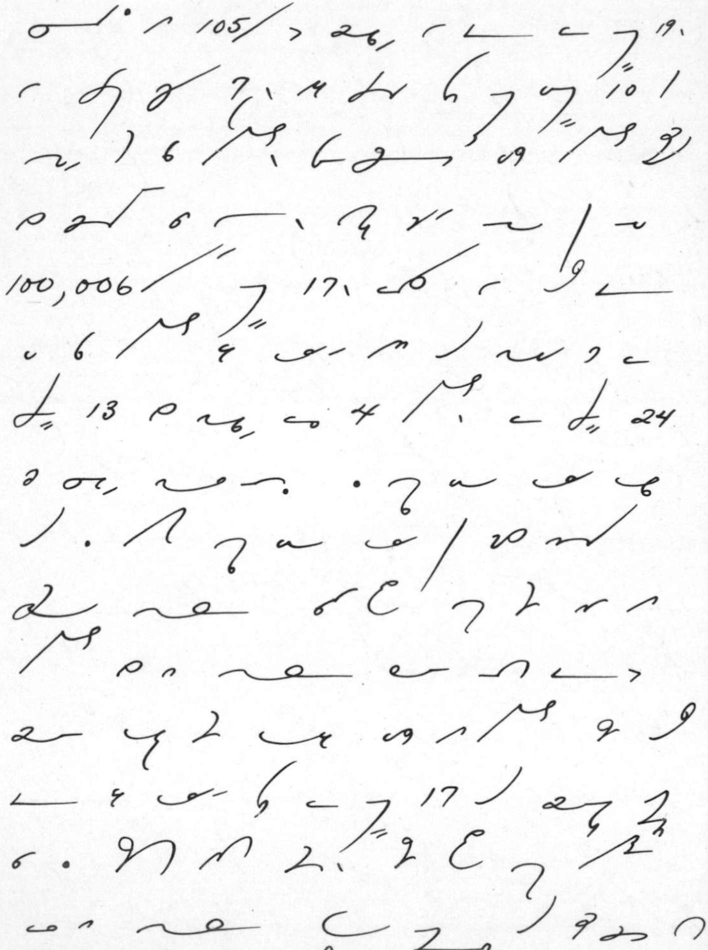

433.

ASSIGNMENT 74

434. Phrase Drill

435. Special-Form Drill

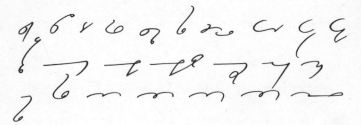

Reading and Writing Exercise

436.

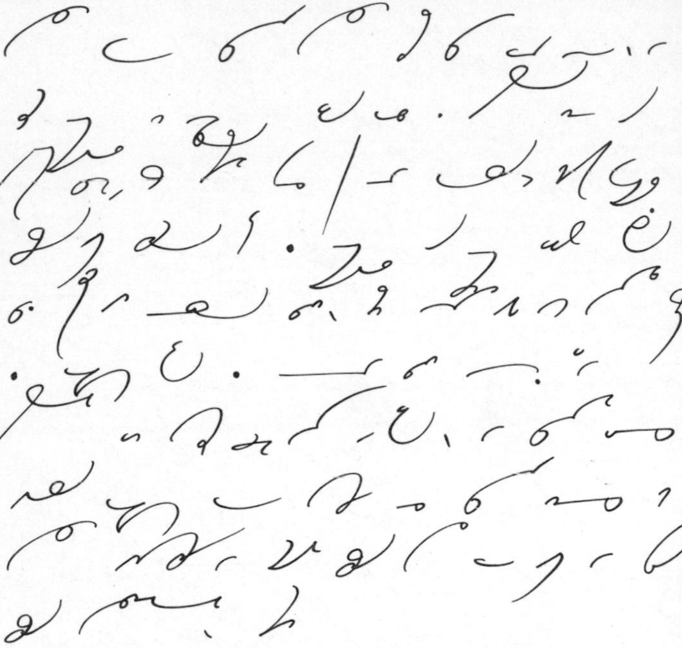

437.

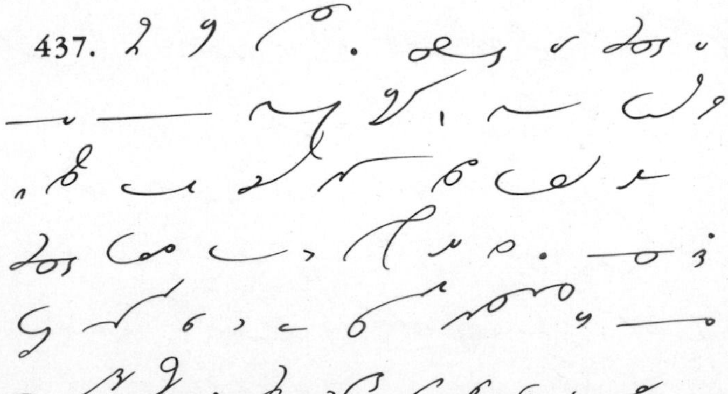

438. Phrase Drill

439. Brief-Form Drill

Reading and Writing Exercise

440.

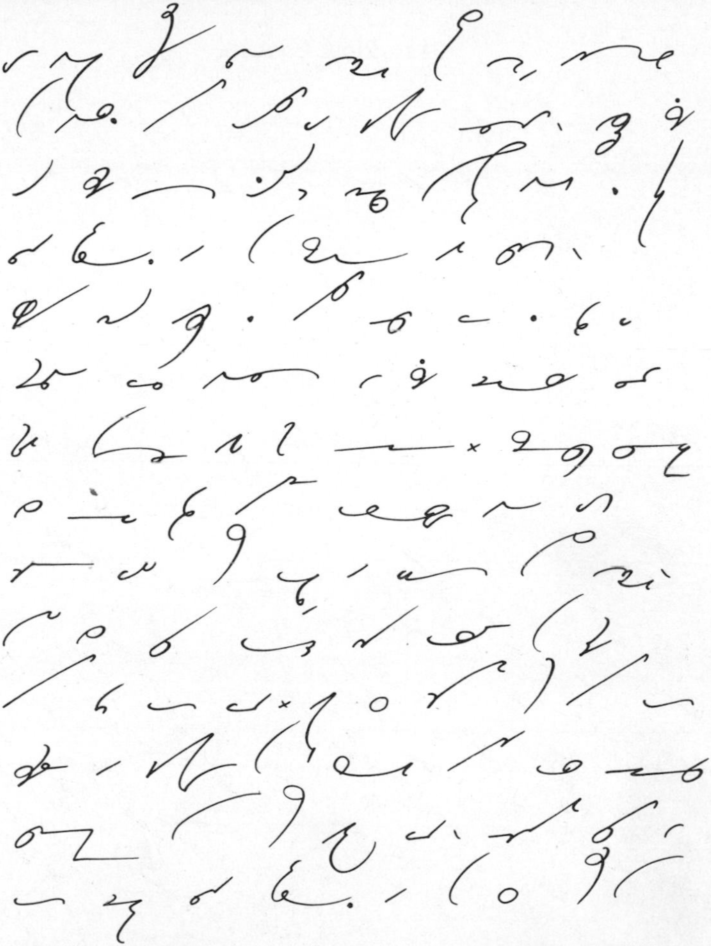

441. How Long?

442. Phrase Drill

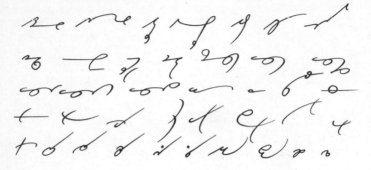

443. Special-Form Drill

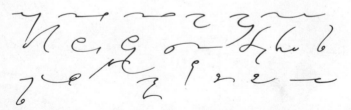

Reading and Writing Exercise

444.

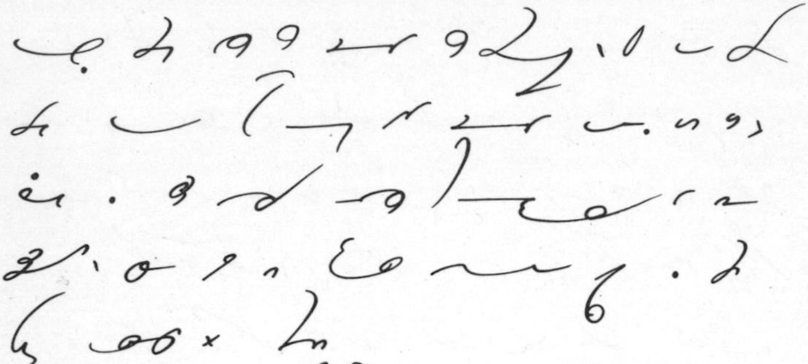

445.

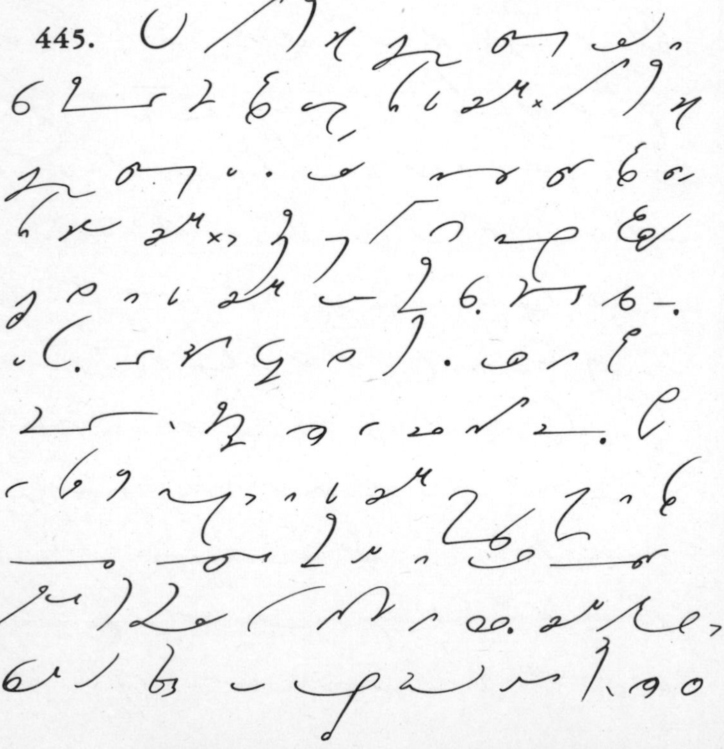

[Shorthand outlines]

446.

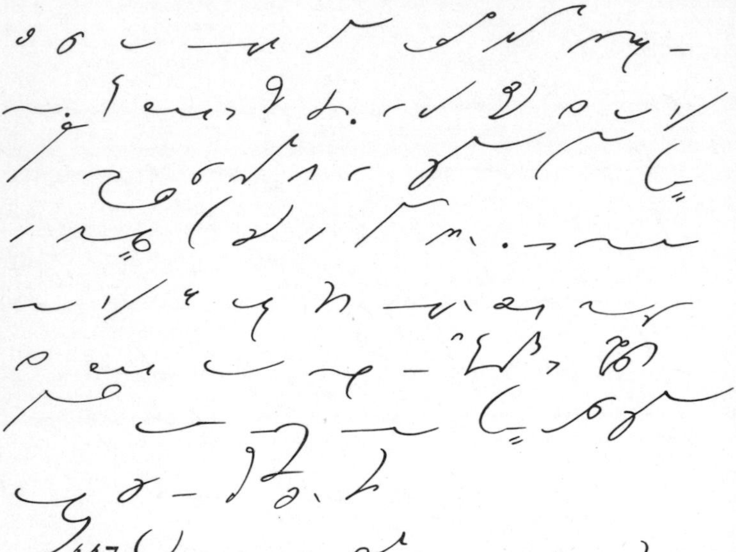

447.

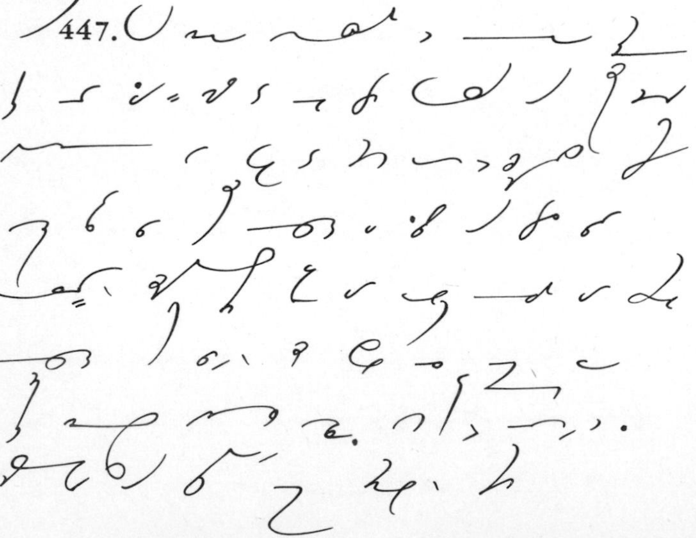

448.

[Shorthand outlines]

Assignment 77

449. Phrase Drill

450. Brief-Form Drill

Reading and Writing Exercise

451.

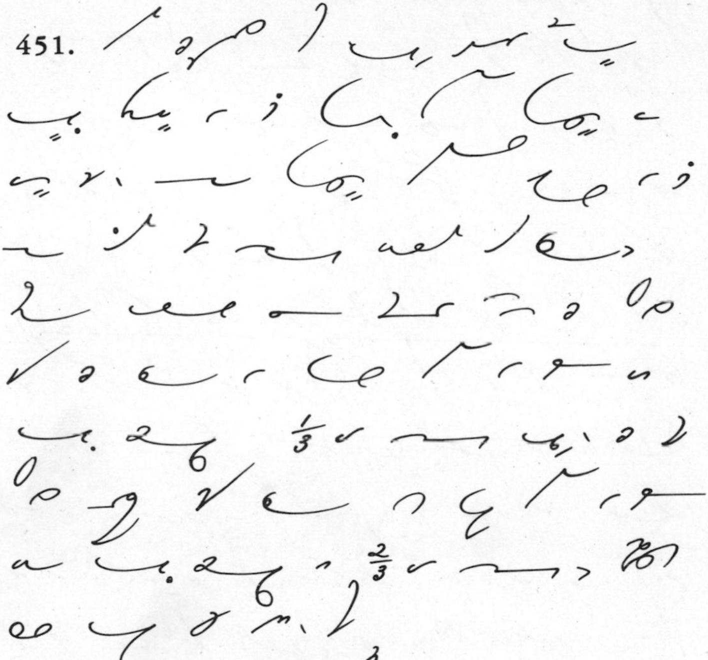

452.

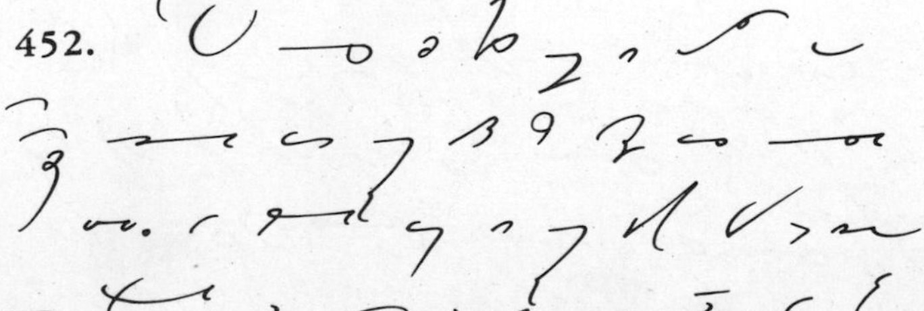

453.

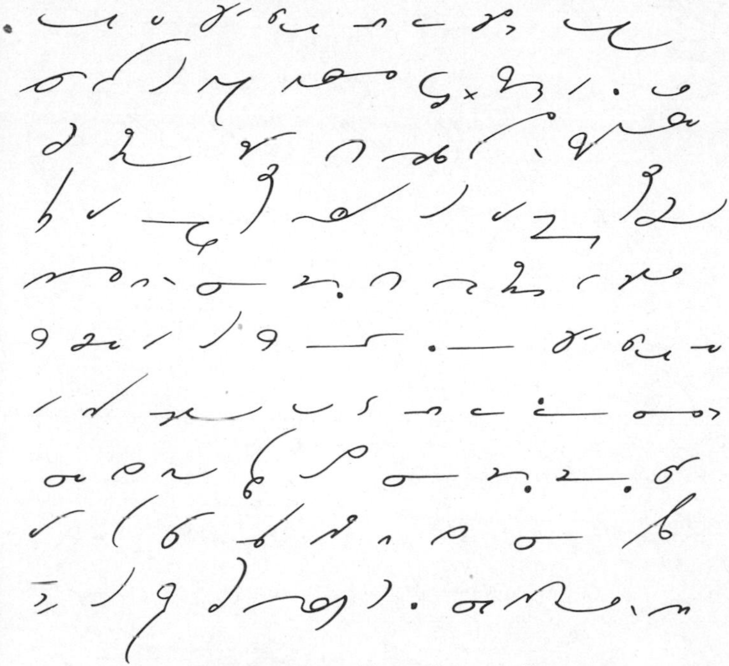

454. THE PRACTICE THAT MAKES PERFECT

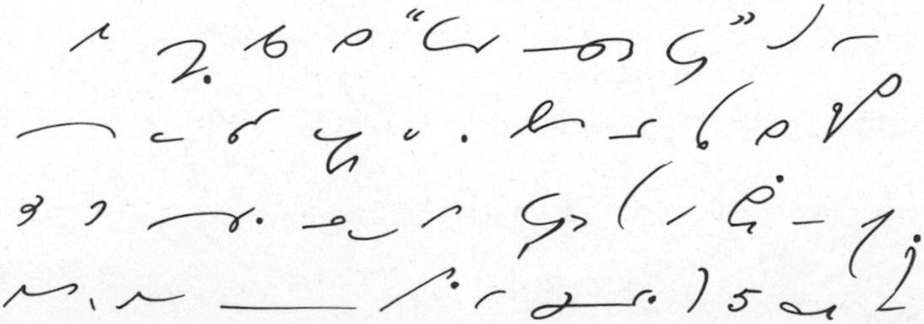

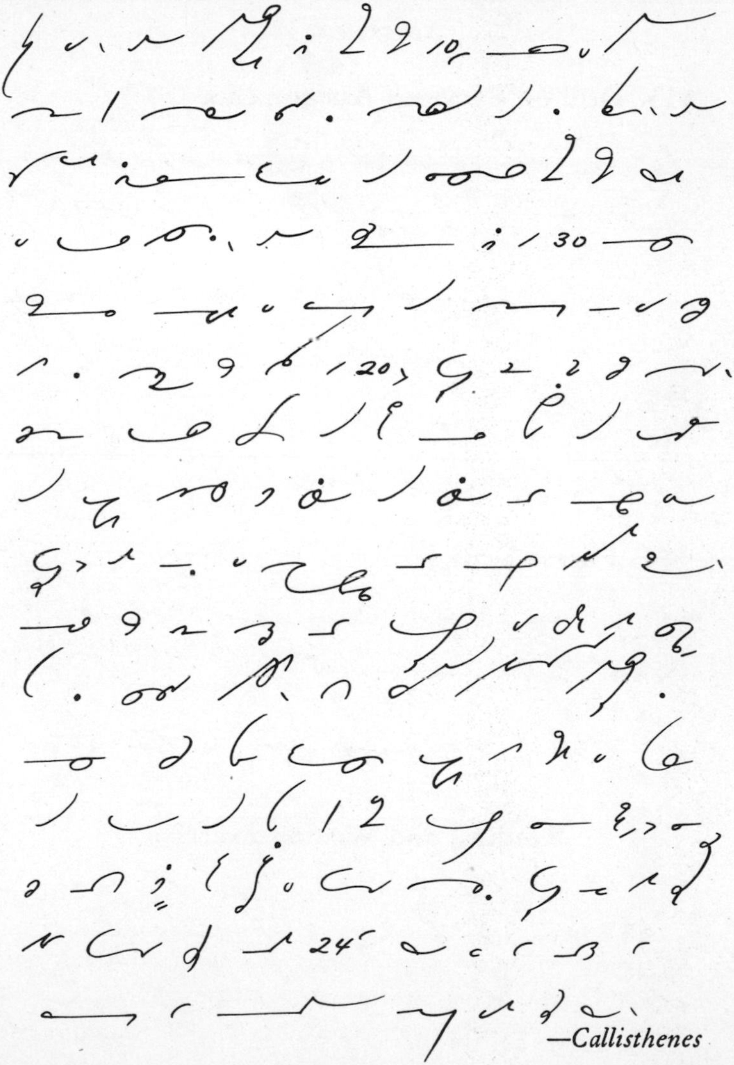

—*Callisthenes*

ASSIGNMENT 78

455. Drill on Previous Assignments

456. Phrase Drill

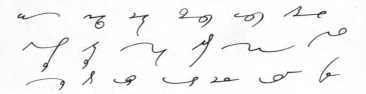

Reading and Writing Exercise

457.

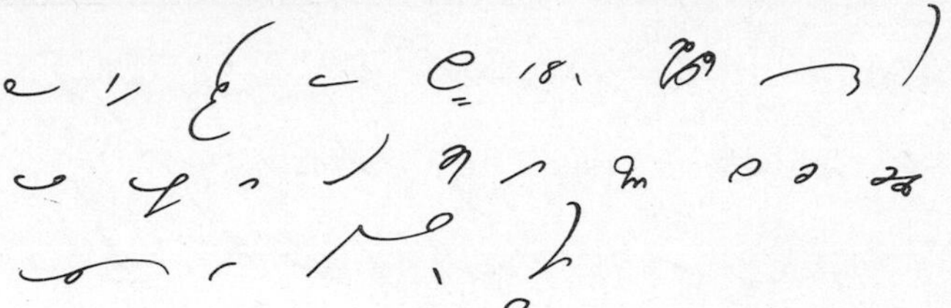

458.

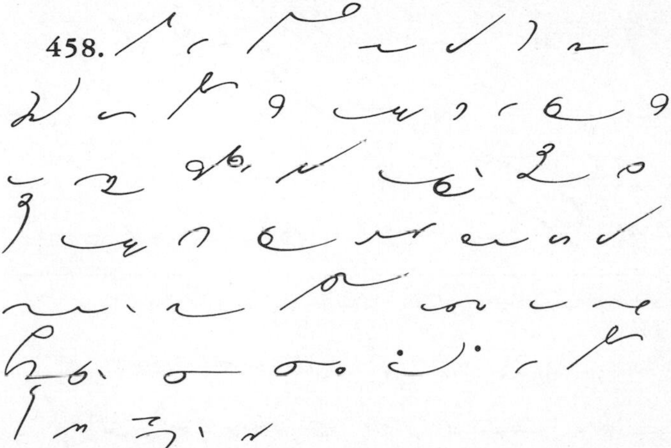

459.

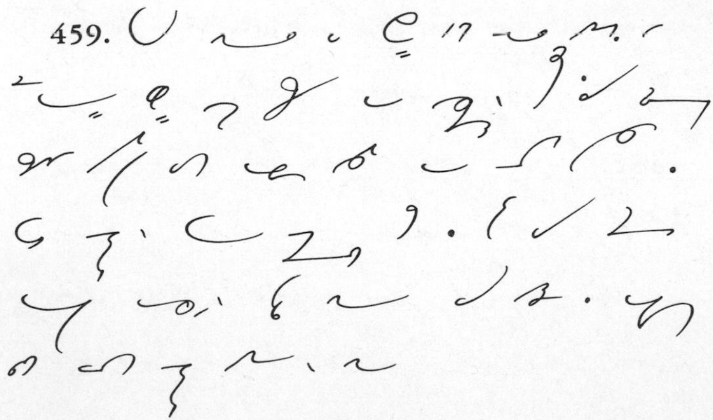

460.

461.

462.

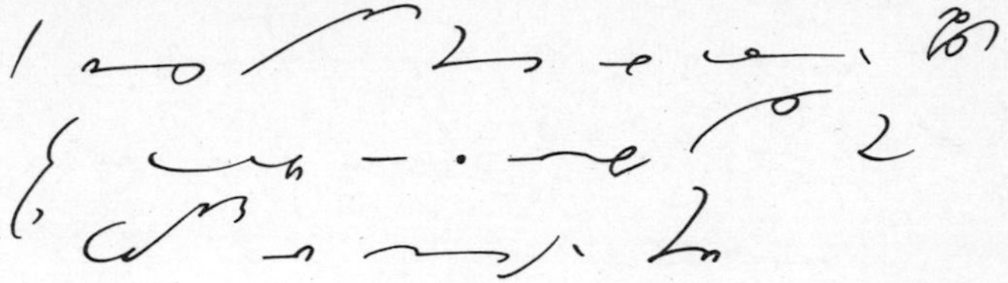

463.

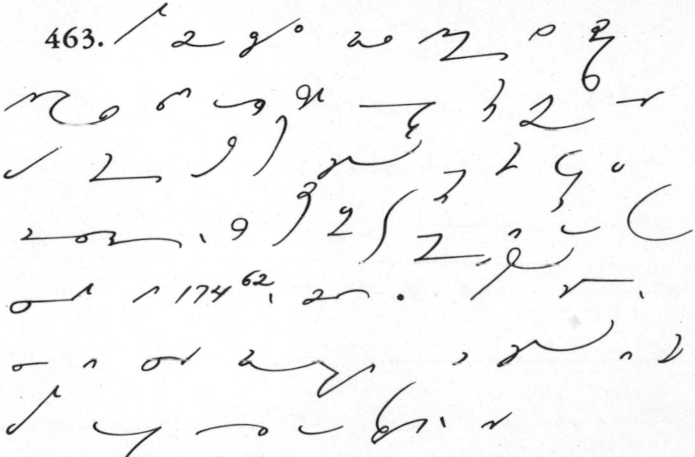

464.

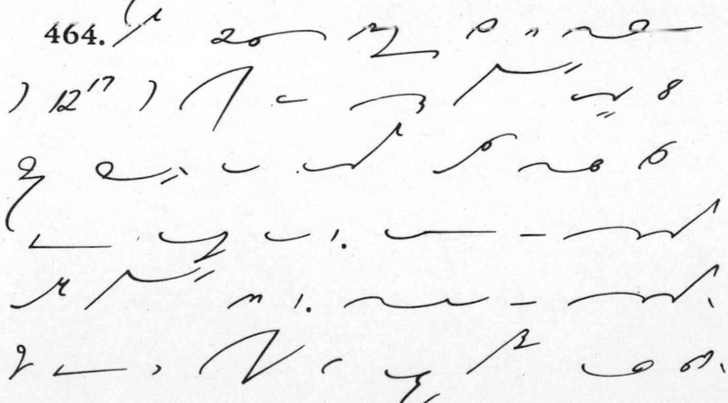

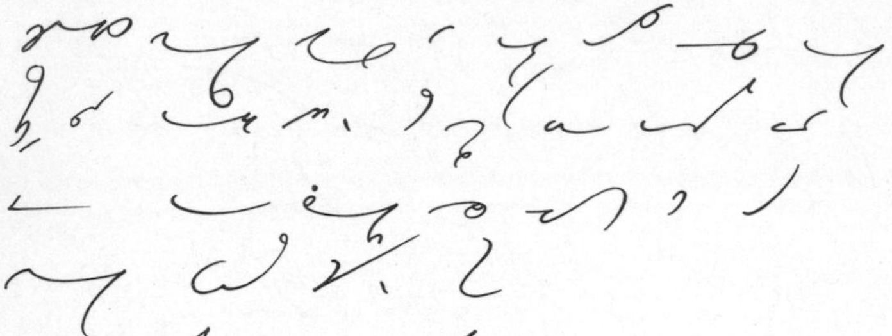

465.

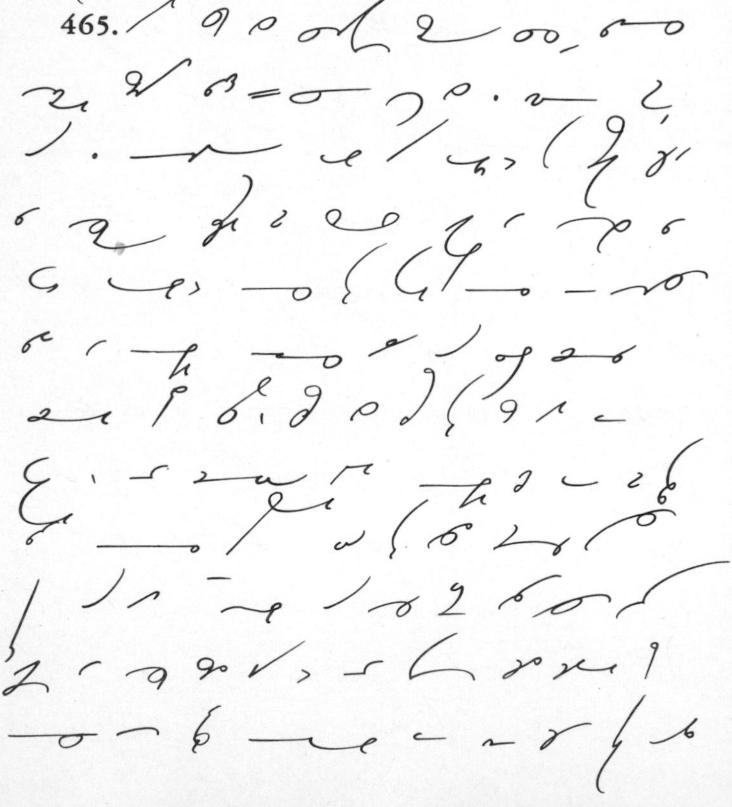

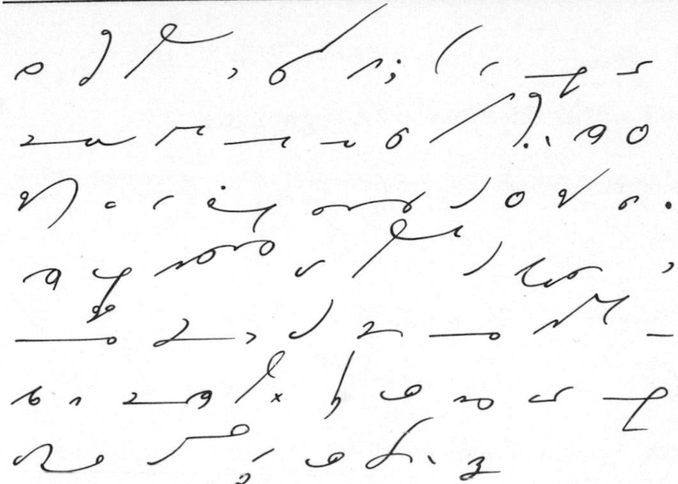

466.

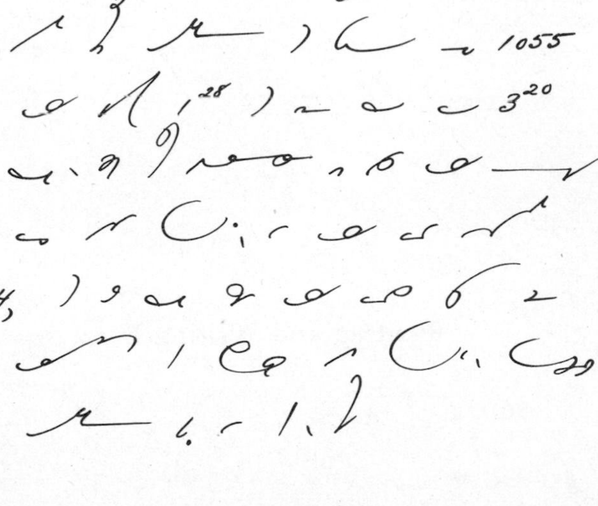

467. Drill on Previous Assignments

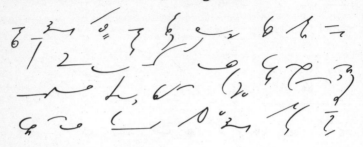

468. Special-Form Drill

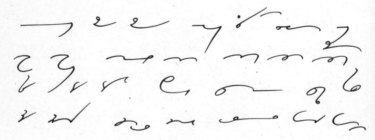

Reading and Writing Exercise

469.

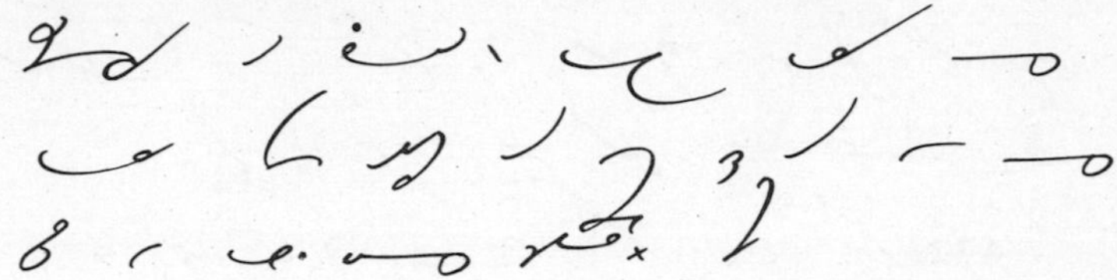

470.

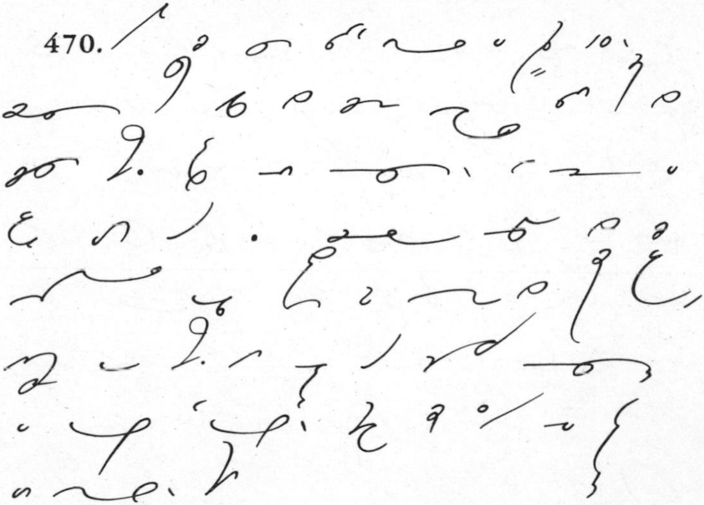

471.

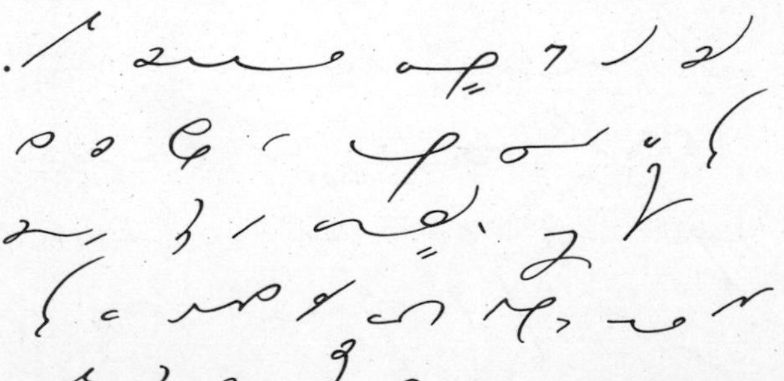

(shorthand outlines)

472.

(shorthand outlines)

473.

(shorthand outlines) $5\frac{1}{2}$

474.

475. Gettysburg Address

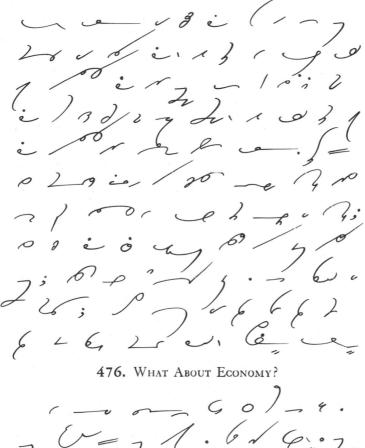

476. What About Economy?

ASSIGNMENT 80

477. Drill on Previous Assignments

478. Brief-Form Drill

Reading and Writing Exercise

479.
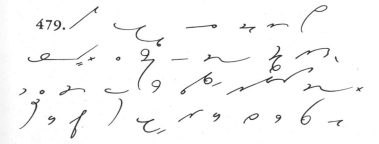

(shorthand outlines)

480. *(shorthand outlines)*

17. *(shorthand outlines)*

481. *(shorthand outlines)*

482. *(shorthand outlines)* 21

(shorthand outlines)

483. *(shorthand outlines)* 15

(shorthand outlines)

484. *(shorthand outlines)* 278 *(shorthand outlines)*

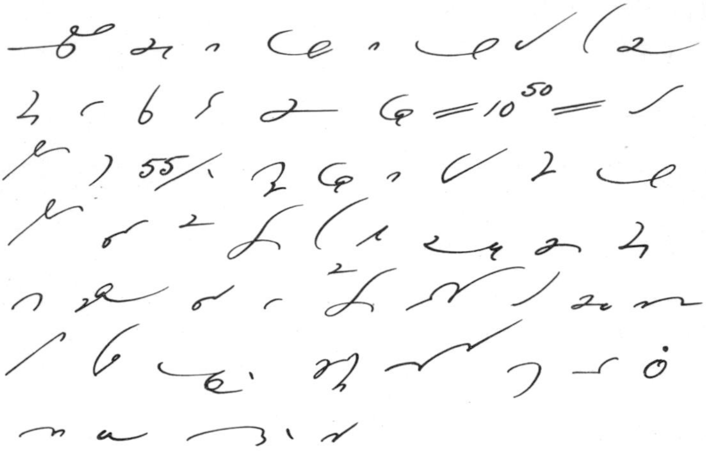

485. The Only Preservative

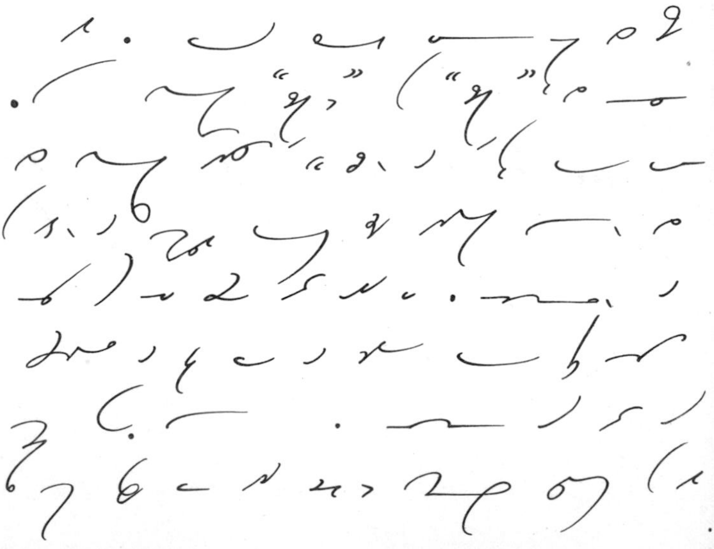

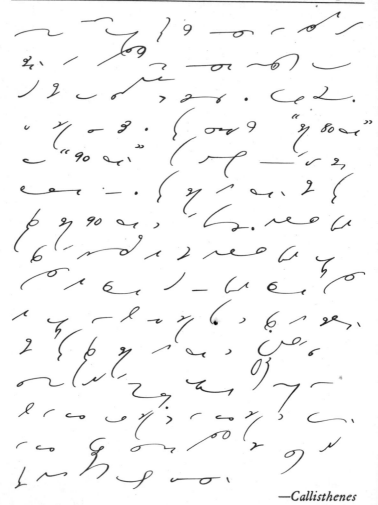

—*Callisthenes*

Used by permission of Selfridge and Company, Ltd., London.

486. Drill on Previous Assignments

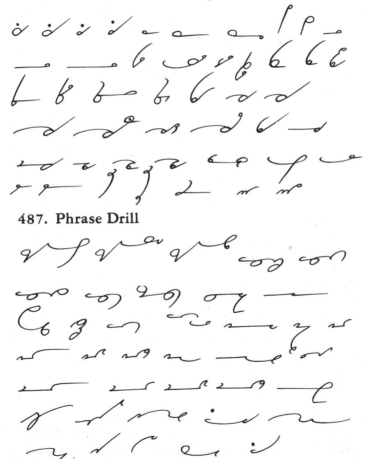

487. Phrase Drill

Reading and Writing Exercise

488.

489.

491.

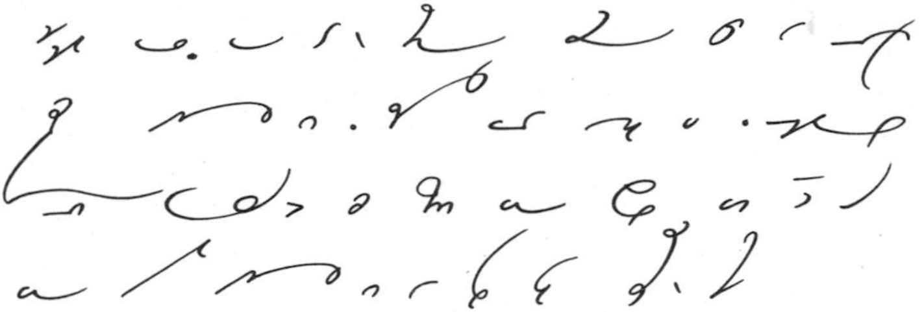

492. Business Habits

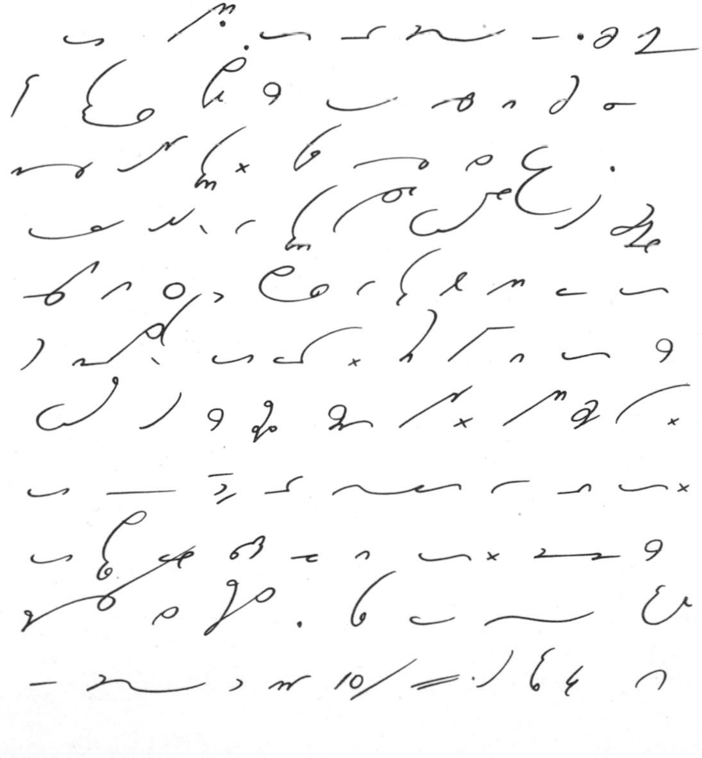

493. THE SECRET BLOTTING PAD

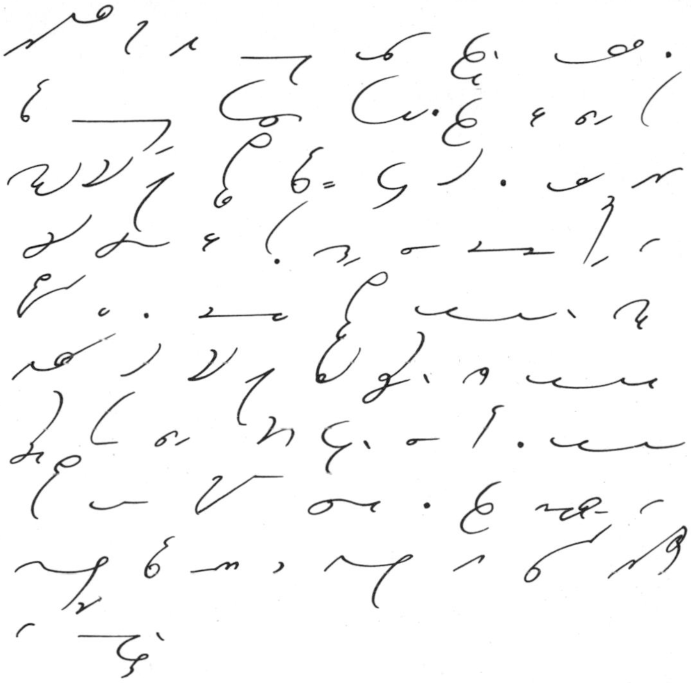

494. Drill on Previous Assignments

Reading and Writing Exercise

495.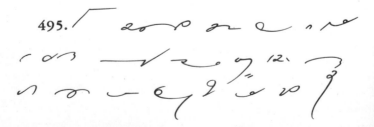

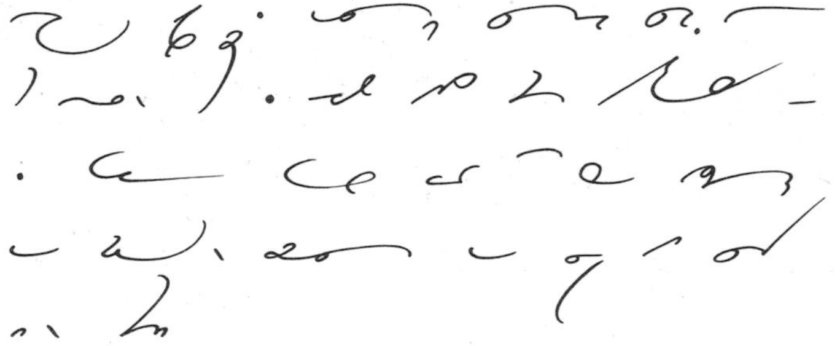

496.

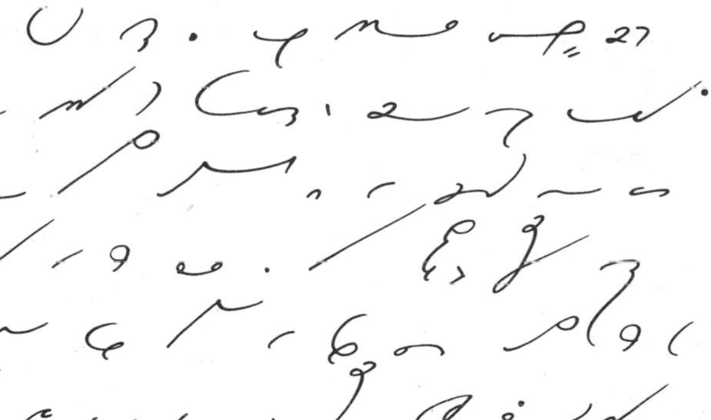

497.

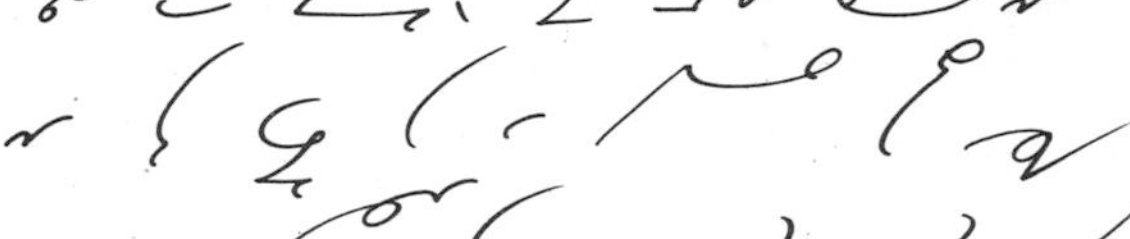

498.

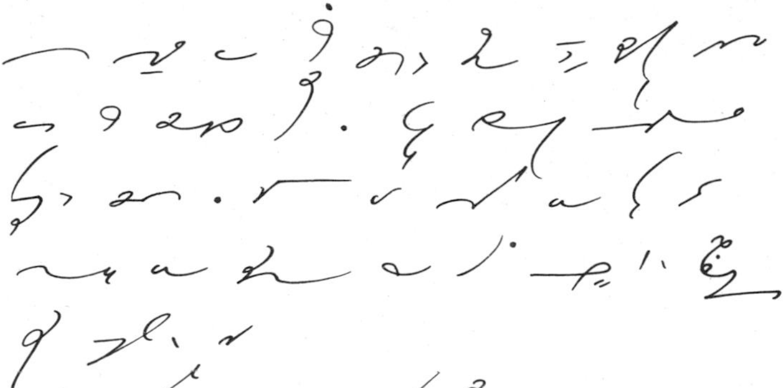

499.

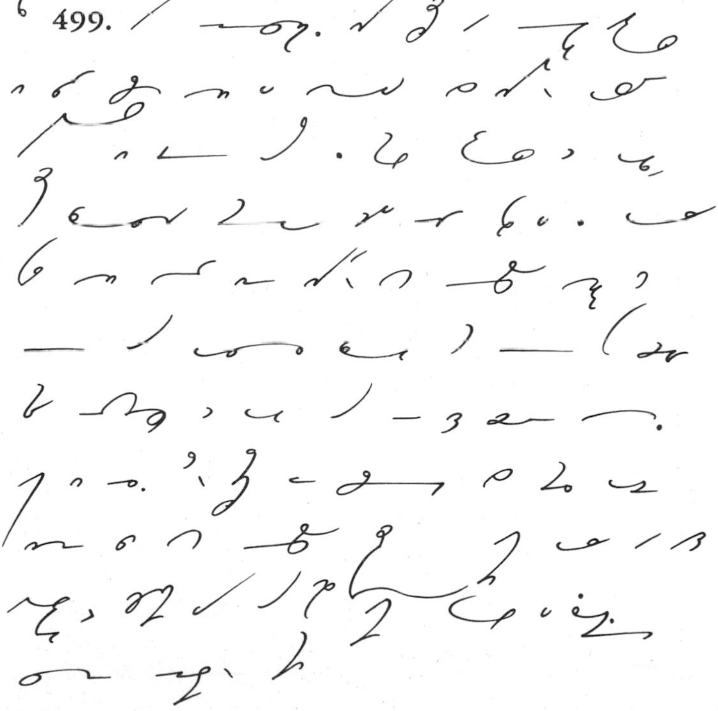

500.

501.

502. Phrase Drill

Reading and Writing Exercise

503.

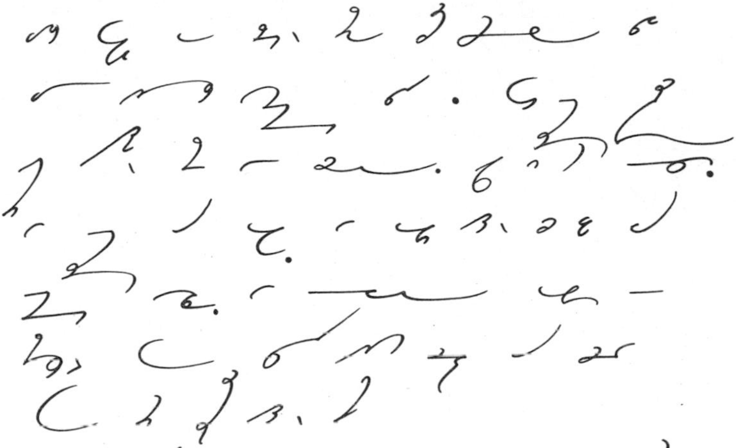

504.

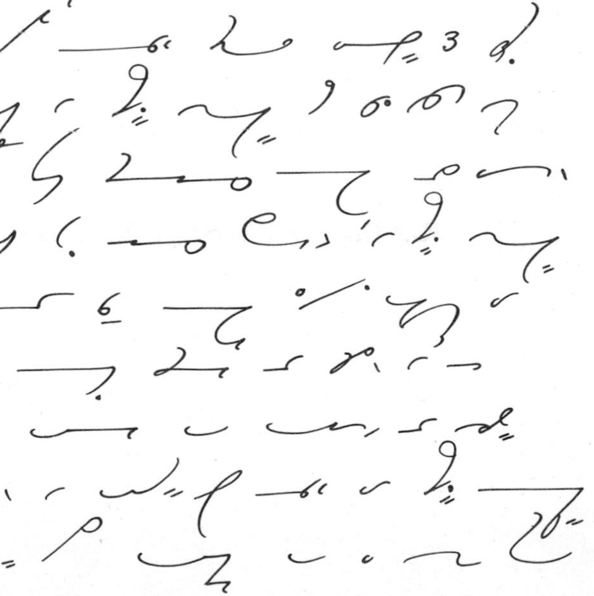

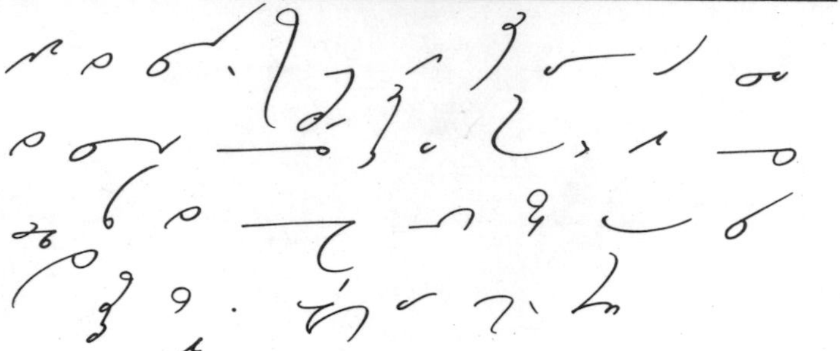

505. 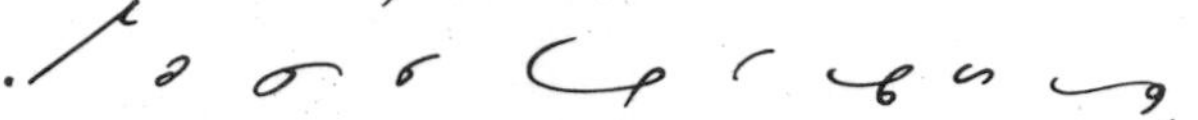

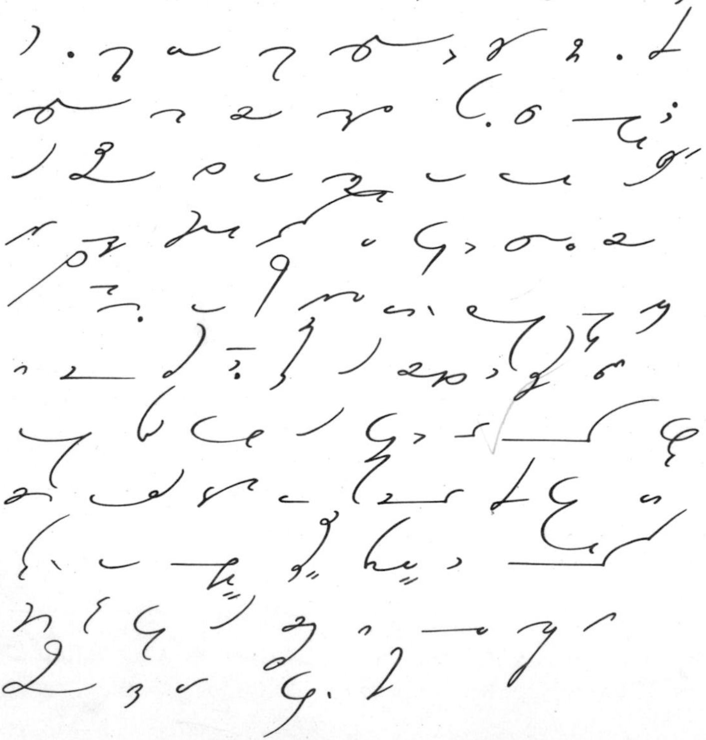

Transcript of Shorthand

CHAPTER VIII

ASSIGNMENT 40

196. I do not believe, they don't, you do not, to make, it may be, at any, at any time, what to do, in due course, I had, you had, who had, it was not, I was not, it is not, it wasn't, he is not, which is not, I am not, sending, unofficial, coming, recourse, discourse.

197. (*a*) Best, rest, test, contest, protest, invest, honest, request, past, last, just, adjust, insist, consist, persist, exist, cost.

(*b*) Act, enact, fact, exact, project, affect, conduct, product, adapt, adopt, evident, student, highest, earliest.

198. Lost, east, fast, cast, vast, least, dust, taste, missed, mixed, post, coast, worst, distant, intent, content, extent, patent.

199. Reading and Writing Exercise

CHOICES

Life consists of choices. We must face the fact that we must forget the past and decide whether we shall build our lives[1] on the highest and finest things or whether we are going to be content to be drifters.

Many honest and[2] well-meaning people persist in being drifters. They fail to realize the fact that they have their lives before them[3] and that the things they do now and the friends they select will affect their future.

There will always be two types of[4] individuals in this world. There will be those who sail and those who drift. The drifters insist that they are content and[5] it is evident by their conduct that they will not accomplish anything useful. They are not the people who[6] undertake the biggest projects. The man who sails knows exactly what to do and knows how to adapt himself to[7] every situation. He may come in contact with difficult problems; he may be put to many tests that[8] will try his patience, but he will keep on trying.

Isn't it a fact that we can accomplish many things if we[9] will just do our very best from day to day and invest the necessary time and effort?

An incident occurred[10] in our school last fall that caused me to think about this matter very seriously. A girl came back to school[11] and enrolled as a student and was determined to finish her education. She is starting her second year[12] of work after having been out of school for exactly ten years. For most of us it would be rather difficult[13] to adjust ourselves to this new situation and do our best work. The girl's guardians insisted that she leave[14] school, and although this seemed to be an unjust request, she yielded without protest.

She has convinced them now, though, that[15] an education is necessary and she is returning to school. She is a charming girl and very modest.[16] It would have been an easy task for her to drift, but I am sure she was justified in returning to school.[17] She says she will not rest until she has gone through college. She realizes that a college education will[18] cost money but whatever it costs it will be a good investment. Here is a girl who is not content to drift.[19]

I know another girl who acts as though she did not care to finish school and was going just because her parents[20] requested her to. The girl could be a very good student, but she has little use for school. The decision she[21] makes now will affect her whole future life.

The world today owes no man a living. It is up to every[22] individual to do the best he can. He must choose a goal and never rest until he reaches it. (457 standard words)

Gentlemen: Paper and ink are two lifeless mediums as they lie on the printer's shelves. But bring them together[1] through the medium of the printing press and you can touch the emotions of millions of human beings. You can[2] delight the eye with any or all the shades of the rainbow or portray the black of night sprinkled with thousands of[3] stars.

Your business message can be just a lifeless piece of paper or it can be a good-looking piece of printing[4]—and printing good-looking advertising pieces is our specialty.

We know how to bring paper and ink together[5] through the skillful use of type faces so as to give your sales message such a form that it will attract attention.[6]

Our direct-mail advertising service is complete. We outline the plans of your campaign, furnish you with[7] suggested layouts, or, if you wish, we write the copy for your various mailing pieces. A sample of our work[8] is enclosed. Everything will be handled and produced by us complete.

We shall be glad to supply you with further[9] details upon request. Yours truly, (166 standard words)

200. Few minutes, years ago, I want, I hope to hear, I hope you can, give him, I am sure, I feel sure, you were, we were, be sure, day or two ago, early reply, at an early date, do you want, I am sorry.

201. Doctrine, emphasize-emphasis, energy, English, entitle, estate, exchange, execute, exercise, familiar, fault, fortune, freight, fulfill, glorious, God.

202. Reading and Writing Exercise

WASTE LAND

On every continent in this world there exist vast tracts of what we call waste land. By waste land we mean places[1] that are not adapted to the growing of grain products on which man could exist. There has been in the past a good[2] deal of this worthless land in the west.

Even though these lands are unsuitable for farming they contain much wealth in[3] the form of minerals. I know several farmers who thought their ground was worthless but then they discovered gold. What[4] a glorious sensation they got when they handled the metal! Right then they began to worry about the best[5] ways of packing the gold for the freight train. Many farmers made a fortune in this way. In the western part of this[6] country there are a number of barren but very valuable tracts of land. Though no farm products can be grown[7] there the land yields much gold and other precious metals.

This country is unfortunate for the great many swamp

lands[8] which are of no value to anybody. The time will come when we shall need that land badly and someone will[9] discover how to get rid of the excess water. When this is accomplished, it will be no trick to change this waste land[10] into valuable farming soil. (206 standard words)

Dear Sir: I am sure I cannot emphasize too strongly the importance of a good English background. A business[1] man must exercise the greatest care in writing letters. He must be familiar with the proper use of business[2] terms so that no possible fault can be found with the letter.

The man who has had special training in business English[3] is indeed fortunate. The man who has had training in our organization is doubly fortunate because[4] he has had the advantage of studying under men whose work has entitled them to a high place in the[5] business world. These men have a good deal of energy and their wide experience makes them ideal teachers.

The textbook[6] used in our course is written by the head of our English department, who is well equipped to speak on business[7] forms and doctrines. The English exercises have been planned so as to give the student the greatest opportunity[8] to do creative work.

Very often students who have studied elsewhere have other English textbooks, and therefore[9] do not care to spend any more money on new books. In cases like these, we are glad to make an exchange so[10] as to save the student further expense.

Our school, as you know, is in the beautiful grounds of an old estate that[11] once belonged to an army officer who was executed in the last war.

As I said, a business man cannot[12] place too much emphasis on English—and what a glorious feeling he has when his letters go out correct[13] in every detail! Come in and talk with us about our English course. Yours truly, (275 standard words)

Dear Sir: This letter will confirm our telephone conversation of yesterday. We shall be glad to have you send[1] the books by freight if they will get here in good shape so that they may be resold as new. You will be given full credit[2] for these books and we shall inform our bookkeeper to that effect.

If the dealer exercises good care in handling[3] the books when they reach him, we are always glad to have him return them for credit or exchange them for some[4] other item that we have in stock.

We cannot emphasize too strongly that we want to do all we can to help[5] you. Yours truly, (102 standard words)

Dear Madam: Thank you for your letter of August 29. Before filling the order, we thought it best to write[1] you about your account. I wonder whether you realize that your previous account for $230[2] is now overdue nearly four months. Perhaps it was overlooked, although we have written you several[3] times about it.

We like to help our friends by giving them credit as long as they need it, but we want to feel[4] that they are working with us and will do everything to take care of the account. I am sure you realize[5] that we cannot meet our own obligations if our friends will not meet theirs.

Please remember that we want your business[6] and that we try to merit it by the quality of the goods and the service we give. We hope, therefore, that you[7] will send us your check for the $230 that is past due. Upon its receipt, we shall give your[8] new order immediate attention.

We know we can depend on you to do all you can to settle this account.[9] Very sincerely yours, (185 standard words)

Assignment 42

203. Doctrine, emphasize-emphasis, fortune, freight, exchanges, executed, exercise, coupons, curious, designate, disagreements, disturbed, default, democrat, deceive, entitled, familiar.

204. Mind, remind, command, demand, intend, extend, pound, expound, compound, beyond, dividend, pretend, diamond.

205. Commend, contend, attend.

206. Admit, admittance, admitted, admiration, adventure, adverse.

207. Admire, advance, advise-advice, I admire, we admire, in advance, I advise, we advise.

208. *(a)* Ultimate, ultimately, ulster, ultimatum. *(b)* Almanac, alter, alternate, alternative, aldermen. *(c)* Submit, substance, subsidy, subway, suburb, subdivide, subdivision, subdue. *(d)* Needless, hopeless, helpless, worthless, homeless, thoughtless, unless, powerless, valueless, useless.

209. Reading and Writing Exercise

A Race with the Clock

The other day I was reminded of an alderman I once met in the subway. I admired the man because[1] he was a good speaker and had a fine command of words. He was very much in demand as an after-dinner[2] speaker and at one dinner that I attended he spoke about "A race with the clock."

He said he was watching[3] a race in the suburbs and he saw everyone with his eyes on a huge clock. The runners realized the value[4] of time and their ultimate goal was to save a fraction of a second. This alderman stressed the value of time[5] and insisted that time once lost can never be regained. Minutes are as precious as diamonds and yet, I am sorry[6] to admit, thoughtless individuals do not seem to mind wasting them.

It is needless to say that things never[7] get done if we only intend to do them. Once we set out to accomplish something nothing should alter our[8] course. Everyone has the same number of hours at his command, but some people make these hours pay richer dividends.[9] Arnold Bennett once said that time is truly a daily wonder. You wake up in the morning with twenty-four hours[10] of time. It is yours and unless you use it you are the loser. Moreover, you cannot draw on the future. You[11] cannot use your allotted time in advance.

Life is a great adventure. There are so many things we should attend[12] to, but our task is hopeless—we have only twenty-four hours a day in which to work. It is an admitted fact[13] that our lives very often are too busy, but we must not submit to that fact as it might easily cause our[14] ultimate ruin.

We must learn to make the most of our time. We must not spend our time reading worthless books and pretending[15] to enjoy them. Take the advice of great educators, who advocate setting aside fifteen or twenty[16] minutes each day for the reading of classics. If possible, extend that time beyond the fifteen or twenty minutes[17]—spend a half hour or an hour each day. You will never regret it.

How few people ever stop to take an[18] inventory of their leisure time to see what they do with the hours that are not spent sleeping, working, or eating. What[19] becomes of all these hours after five or six, when work is over? Are they used in a commendable way or must[20] we admit that we let them drop into the past without their having added one thing to improve our mind or body?[21]

Any plan of using one's spare moments that will increase his knowledge or broaden his outlook is a good plan.[22] But how many hours and minutes are wasted every day in fruitless and useless conversation and in profitless[23] amusement!

If we want to be a success, we must make a profitable use of our spare time—we have no[24] alternative. (482 standard words)

Dear Madam: You are a very important person to me, for you are among the very few people who have[1] not ordered anything from us during the past year. I must admit I am wondering why.

Your experience[2] with us has surely proved that we bring to you the very latest styles and that our goods are the finest obtainable.[3] You know that our prices are the lowest in the country. That is the opinion of countless thousands of women[4] who demand the best for the least money.

In view of this, you can see that I am rather concerned for the loss[5] of your good will. If we have failed to satisfy you in some way, give me an opportunity to make whatever[6] adjustments are necessary. If, though, you have not visited us simply because you have not had occasion[7] to buy from us, please put our minds at ease by mailing the enclosed card.

We shall, naturally, continue to[8] send you our monthly fashion bulletin. I believe that our summer issue, which appears in April, will be more[9] helpful than ever, for we have added a number of new departments that will greatly increase our opportunities[10] for being of service to you.

May I ask a personal favor? Please answer the two questions on the[11] enclosed sheet and return the sheet to me in the enclosed envelope. Just this small effort on your part will be a[12] wonderful aid in my endeavor to be of service to you. Cordially yours, (254 standard words)

Gentlemen: Thank you for your recent cash order, for which we are indeed grateful. I wonder whether you wouldn't[1] care to take advantage of an open account with us. I have spoken to the credit manager and it will[2] be perfectly satisfactory to him.

You may wish to deal with us for some reason on a strictly cash basis,[3] but we want you to know that your credit is good with us. Yours truly, (72 standard words)

Assignment 43

210. Presented, depart, matters, causes, myself, times truthful, charges, discharge, expression, girlish, doctors, called, believed, wanted, namely, forgave, begs, thinking.

211. Headquarters, husband, inasmuch, inaugurate, independent-independence, indispensable, institute, investigate, junior, jury, legislate, legislation, legislative, legislator, legislature, likewise.

212. Reading and Writing Exercise

Dear Sir: The package containing a fountain pen and two pencils reached my headquarters this morning. Inasmuch as[1] these things were marked for my attention, I examined them personally, but I could find nothing wrong with the pen.[2] Therefore, I am returning it to you with the request that you give it another trial. I shall have the two pencils[3] replaced. I know you will find them indispensable in your work.

As you have ordered these pencils from time to[4] time, you will be glad to hear that we are now selling them for $1.40 a dozen. We are selling[5] them at this low price as we intend to discontinue their sale after December 31. The pencils[6] have been selling rapidly since we made this special price, but we still have a small supply left.

The man who has charge[7] of the supplies in the state legislature bought a gross of the pencils. He said that the legislators and the[8] members of the investigating committees liked these pencils very much.

If you care to have any of these[9] pencils and will send us a remittance for as many as you want, I shall see that you get them. Very truly[10] yours, (201 standard words)

Dear Madam: You say that the charges for delivery of your paper have been high. Some time ago you asked us[1] to send this paper by the Independent Express Company, which we did. I have investigated the cost[2] of sending this paper by freight and I find the rates very reasonable. Perhaps in the future it may be[3] wise to send all this paper by freight.

Enclosed you will find several samples of paper we received recently.[4] Your husband asked me to mail these to him as soon as they came in. Yours truly, (92 standard words)

Dear Mr. Jones: My client wants me to institute a suit against the man who wrecked his car. I wonder whether[1] you would be good enough to investigate the case for me, so that I may have sufficient facts to present to[2] the jury.

The mishap took place on Fifth Avenue, and the car was driven by a young man who is a junior[3] in college. Naturally, I must have all the facts about the mishap, the statements of the various witnesses,[4] and all that sort of thing. As you are an experienced investigator, I am sure you will know what facts[5] are necessary to make out a case.

If you will come in to see me soon, perhaps we can arrange for your fee.[6] Also, I should like your advice on some minor points having to do with the trial of the case before a judge and[7] jury. Very truly yours, (145 standard words)

Dear Reader: For many years we have been aware of the fact that book readers intend to join the Book Club but then[1] put it off and soon forget about it. In order to spur you on to join immediately, we are going[2] to make it very much worth your while: If you will join the Book Club within the next thirty days, we will present you[3] with a copy of "The First Inauguration." The book is bound in beautiful leather and is printed on the[4] finest paper obtainable. It deals with the days when our country was first fighting for its independence. It[5] tells how the Constitution was framed and how the legislative and other branches of our Government were[6] organized. Likewise, it tells of the troubles the fathers of our country had during the first days that they started to[7] legislate. The framers of our Constitution gave great thought to new legislation.

A copy of "The First[8] Inauguration" will be sent to you if you sign the enclosed card and return it within thirty days. Sincerely[9] yours, (181 standard words)

Dear Mr. Smith: Frankly, as one business man to another, I have come to ask a small favor of you. I wonder[1] if you would be willing to furnish us with the names and addresses of four or five friends who you believe would[2] like to find out about the kind of banking services we try to give to the people of our city.

I do[3] not mind telling you that we should place these names on our list, sending them the printed matter that we issue, and thus[4] try to make them our friends. Of course we should not think of using your name in this connection unless you are willing.[5]

Would it not be a source of satisfaction to you if you could put on that list the name of someone to whom a[6] bank account would be a blessing—someone who has not yet been awakened to the importance of laying aside[7] a little out of every month's pay for that rainy day that is sure to come? Thus your service to our bank may become[8] a real service to a fellow citizen.

May we have the pleasure of hearing from you soon? Yours truly, (179 standard words)

Assignment 44

213. Represents, expresses, employee, carefully, carries, forceful, discharged, belong, longed, returning, answerable, useful, outing, disappointment, inquiries, wires, wonders.

214. In the world, ought to be, more or less, little or no, one or two, week or two, some of them, some of those, ought to have, for the time being, question of time, out of the question, one of the most, sooner or later, in a week or two, in reference to the matter, in regard to the matter, up to the time, on the subject, that is to say, able to say, more and more, little or nothing, in a day or two, I should like to have.

215. Reading and Writing Exercise

Dear Sir: In a week or two I shall send you one of the most valuable certificates you have ever[1] received. I should like to have an opportunity to present this to you personally, but for the time being[2] that is out of the question. If you can't use it, sooner or later, please tear it up. It will be little or no[3] trouble for you to fill out the two or three questions asked on that certificate and return it to this office.[4] As soon as we receive the certificate, we shall mail you one of the fine sets of books we are giving as gifts[5] to our friends.

During more than forty years, our publication, "The Review," has been a stronger attraction to[6] distinguished men and women than any other publication in the world. Some of these people have been on our list for more[7] than a quarter of a century. I am able to say that at least fifty have received our publication[8] for thirty-five years.

When we tell our friends that we are going to do a certain thing they know our promise[9] can be depended upon because we have always kept our word. Yours truly, (193 standard words)

Dear Sir: Thank you for your letter of several days ago in regard to the matter of desks. I am sorry[1] we cannot send you these desks for a week or two, as we are entirely out of stock of the model you want. I[2] have written to the factory in reference to the matter of getting more desks and they promise us that in[3] a day or two they can begin work on them.

The demand for these desks is becoming more and more pressing and we[4] are having difficulty filling orders. We were more or less surprised that this model should sell so readily.[5]

That is to say, we knew it was a fine model, but we had rather expected our model 116[6] to sell more rapidly.

If you are in urgent need of these desks, why not try the 116? It ought to[7] be satisfactory, as there is very little difference between that model and the one you requested[8] in your letter. You have little or nothing to lose by giving this 116 model a trial—we shall[9] be glad to have you try it at our expense.

While we are on the subject of desks, I should like to have you examine[10] the enclosed catalogue. You ought to have one of these catalogues, as it shows the models that are used in[11] different offices throughout the country. Very truly yours, (230 standard words)

Dear Sir: Your boy has probably heard quite a bit about our school this summer from his new friends in camp, and I am[1] sure you too will want to know something of the school those boys represent.

Here each boy is an individual whose[2] progress is limited solely by the effort he is willing to put forth. Each boy's studies are fitted to his[3] needs. The classes are small, averaging about twelve boys to each teacher, so that each individual recites[4] several times daily. In this way the teacher can keep in close touch with all the students.

The new building just opened[5] is the last word in modern equipment. It has one of the most beautiful swimming pools to be found in any[6] school. The school rooms have plenty of light and air and sunshine. We encourage all boys to take part in sports. We have[7] excellent coaches for football, baseball, and other sports.

Come in to visit us and see for yourself what a fine[8] school we have here. If you can't find time to come in, just return the enclosed card and we will send you one of our[9] catalogues. We should like to have you leaf through it. Very truly yours, (191 standard words)

Dear Sir: You ought to be here in a week or two in order to see what we are placing on the market. I am[1] of the opinion that you will have many suggestions on the subject of our advertising, and I should like[2] to have you work hand in hand with me. My son-in-law will be at the office in a day or two, and we can get[3] his advice on the question.

One of the best suggestions I have received so far is that we mail one of our[4] catalogues to the people on our mailing list. We had not planned on doing this, but I know these people will be glad[5] to see them. We have prepared the catalogue in such a manner that it will be little or no trouble to order[6] any of the goods listed.

Please wire me immediately in reference to the matter, as I should like[7] to know what to expect. Yours truly, (146 standard words)

Dear Mr. Jones: I am sure you can realize how pleased I was the other day when the manager of my[1] department complimented me on my last year's record. The credit, though, is not mine, for without the assistance which[2] you and my other clients have given me I should never have been able to make such a good showing. I am[3] planning, with your assistance, to accomplish even more this year.

I want to increase my usefulness to my clients[4] and to continue to help them plan their investments wisely and safely. Very truly yours, (96 standard words)

Assignment 45

216. Smart, lard, guarantee, merit, period, thermometer, cart, art, garden, burn, burner, large, learn, march, worse, deserve, board.

217. Literary, literature, litigation, locate, luxury, manufacture, merchant, messenger, misdemeanor, mortgage, neglect, negligence, negligent, negotiate, novelty, observe.

218. Reading and Writing Exercise

Gentlemen: I have never before had an opportunity to address a group of manufacturers, and[1] I confess I am enjoying the novelty of it. In a sense, though, I think I can claim to be one of you,[2] as I have had occasion to get first-hand knowledge touching your particular industry. Some years ago I[3] set up house as a manufacturer and local merchant, and I did get a good deal of experience, but[4] that is all.

I soon discovered that if a manufacturer wants to pay the mortgage and eat three times a day[5] he has to hustle out and get business and collect bills, and I observed that I was getting very hungry. Though[6] I did not neglect the business for a second, it went from bad to worse. But in this day and age the business[7] experience was worth every penny it cost me. I have never since had the urge to invade your field, but I feel[8] I am speaking about a subject on which I have first-hand knowledge.

To anyone who has not been negligent[9] in reading the literary efforts of present-day writers, it is quite plain that there is no limit to what[10] we may expect. Modern methods and modern machinery have greatly increased production and added to the[11] luxuries that we may now enjoy. These methods have built up a commercial nation second to none. Our literature[12] tells us that in the days gone by history used to confer its choicest favors upon the soldier, but[13] now it confers them upon the business man. There are some who wonder whether this is for the best; who wonder whether[14] we haven't simply built up a machine without a heart. I have heard this view expressed in negotiations[15] of many kinds, and we should recognize that it exists. For my part, I think it is not the proper point of view[16] to take. Some people are always afraid of something new and big. To them anything that is big is bad.

Today[17] we are moving at a rapid rate—it may be too rapid. Our messengers may be found all over the world, spreading[18] our goods wherever they go. At the rate we are going, the time will come when we will be able to go no[19] further—we will have reached our limit. It is well to have a goal, but we must not reach it too quickly—and we must[20] be careful that we do not fall in an attempt to overreach it. (412 standard words)

Dear John: I am sorry it will be necessary for you to appear in court on Monday to defend the young[1] man who is charged with having committed a misdemeanor.

You need not feel bad about it, though, as I, too, will[2] have to be in court on that day. One of my best clients was haled into court because of his negligence in driving[3] a car, and he wants me to take care of the litigation for him. From the facts he has given me, he himself[4] was not negligent and, therefore, I should have no difficulty in trying the case. The plaintiff is a wealthy[5] local manufacturer and has hired several fine lawyers to handle his side of the litigation,[6] but I do not think he will get anywhere.

I hope you are successful in your efforts to defend the young man[7] who is held on a misdemeanor charge. Be sure to keep a careful record of what goes on, so that you may appeal[8] to the higher court if the case is decided against you.

In view of the fact that we cannot meet this Monday,[9] why don't you have dinner with me on Tuesday? Yours truly, (190 standard words)

Dear Mr. Jones: Beginning at noon today, we have a new manager of our local office. When you have[1] recovered from the shock, I shall tell you his name. If you will look closely at the end of this letter, you will find it[2] attached thereto. Perhaps you have guessed it anyway.

Since last May, I have divided my time here at headquarters[3] between learning my job and keeping in touch with you and the rest of the men. I have had every phase of the business[4] under observation, and I have not neglected any branch of our work. I have drilled myself in the routine[5] of the organization, and I can tell you in detail the work of every man on the force, all the[6] way from the messenger to the head accountant. I do not intend to tell you how to go about your business[7]—you know that best. Start the ball rolling now and keep it rolling. It is now December. By next December or[8] January, when the new manager makes his report, we shall know whether he is worth his salt.

I ask your assistance.[9] Cordially yours, (183 standard words)

CHAPTER IX

Assignment 46

219. Gentle, diligent, defeat, endeavor, defer, regent, divide, bond, planned, trained, claimed, profound, contain, stencil, item.

220. Arrive-arrival, derive, engage, strike, grade, trade, doubt, crowd, proud, stood, loud, south, poor, pure, cure, peculiar, confuse, excuse, refuse, became, light, private, glorious, invite, provide, proceed, decide, prevail, repeat, operate.

221. Amount, balance, boulevard, discount, magazine, England, memorandum, post office, equivalent, America, R.R., O.K., free on board, paid, Street, horse power, U.S., U.S.A., ultimo, etc.

222. Reading and Writing Exercise

A Trip to Mexico

There is a saying, "What does one know of America who knows only the United States?" To the south lies[1] Mexico, which is undoubtedly much less known to the people of the United States of America than such[2] an important country should be.

As soon as one arrives on the other side of the border, he perceives a striking[3] difference in the dress and the manner of living of the people. In the crowded cities we find that the[4] people have kept step more or less with civilization. In the native villages, however, the poor people[5] still live exactly as the natives lived many years ago.

Many private homes are made of a very poor grade[6] of wood, and when one is invited to go inside it is difficult to decide whether it is more comfortable[7] lying on the floor or on the bed. As the visitor proceeds further into the country, he observes[8] the peculiar methods that prevail in the farming sections. Most of the natives are engaged in some sort of farming[9] from which they derive enough money to meet their immediate needs. Many of their products are sent to the[10] United States and England. Our trade with Mexico amounts to millions of dollars. It is easy to get the[11] produce of Mexico to the United States, of course, as there are many railroads in operation from that[12] country to this. Some of the products are sent f.o.b. the different United States post offices. Most of[13] the products are paid for immediately.

All the natives of the different villages await the arrival[14] of the train and crowd around it when it arrives.

There is a loud yell from the children as a man tosses them[15] a penny. The lucky child who recovers the penny proudly displays it and waits for another opportunity[16] to repeat his success.

There is a man waiting there who will be delighted to carry your trunk down the[17] boulevard. There is no use looking for an excuse to refuse to let him carry it, because there is no taxi[18] available to take the trunk for you. This strong man is cheerfully paid the small amount he asks for his[19] services. Men and women stand near the railroad and sell bright blankets and provide the visitor with magazines, books,[20] etc. You soon learn that the price of these things is slightly more than you care to pay, and you try to prevail upon[21] them to accept less. Repeatedly they refuse, until the train starts moving. Then they decide to let you have[22] it at your price.

The food these people balance in baskets on their heads does not look inviting. However, the natives[23] have a good appetite, and pure food means nothing to them.

Some of the natives do not hesitate to trade with[24] a live chicken. It is not an unusual sight to see a native march through a train in all his glory with[25] a frightened chicken, weighing far more than a pound, under his arm. The railroad depot is almost the equivalent[26] of one of our food markets.

The "Main Street" presents a peculiar appearance. On each side there is a wall in[27] which every so often there is a door. It would undoubtedly be confusing for us to find our own private[28] residence, as there are no numbers on the doors. On the "Main Street" much trading takes place. All trading is on a cash[29] basis, and there are no unpaid bills. The seller keeps no memorandum of his purchases and sales.

The natives[30] are friendly people, and no matter how crowded their houses may be, they do not use this fact as an excuse to[31] refuse food and shelter to those who are related to them.

Mexico has been accused of being a country[32] full of bandits. There are a few bandits living in the hills, but most of the natives lead a quiet life and are[33] polite and friendly to the visitor. (667 standard words)

ASSIGNMENT 47

223. Greatest, marketable, systems, business men, matters, mornings, letters, gives, forgotten, nameless, statement, committees, represented, valuable, enforcement, carrying, forces.

224. Authentic, capable, certificate, convenience-convenient, cooperate, custom, deposit, develop, duplicate, establish, financial, illustrate-illustration, imagine-imagination, language, length, liberty, material, offer, original, pleasant, popular, policy, prejudice, principle, relative, privilege, travel, union.

225. Obstruct, obvious, occupy-occupation, Pacific, parcel, partial, passenger, patron, pattern, persecute, plaintiff, practical, practice, premium, probability, property.

226. Reading and Writing Exercise

Dear Sir: I am indeed sorry that it will not be convenient for me to see you on Christmas Day, as we had[1] originally planned. As you know, the Pacific Insurance Company holds a reunion for its officers[2] every year at this time, and it is customary for each office to cooperate and send delegates.[3] This year it is my privilege to go as a delegate, and I was pleasantly surprised when I received[4] the offer.

Elaborate plans have been made, and there are several capable men as the principal speakers.[5] I am sure I will receive practical advice on how to handle some of our patrons.

I have developed a[6] liking for flying, and whenever possible I travel by plane. Obviously this practice saves a great deal[7] of time. Mr. Allen will be a passenger on our plane, and he will occupy the seat in front of me.

I[8] am anxious to talk with him about the financial situation of the Brown case in which he was one of the[9] plaintiffs. I took the liberty of attending the preliminary hearings, at which time I met Mr. Allen's[10] lawyer. This lawyer is considered one of the most brilliant and clever men in the state.

It is obvious[11] that the jury was prejudiced and partial, or it would have decided in favor of Mr. Allen. Cordially[12] yours, (241 standard words)

Dear Sir: Since you are not yet familiar with the work we are doing in your state, I will write you at some length on[1] the points that will, in all probability, cause you trouble. I am confident that you are capable of handling[2] the work, but there are several men who will do their best to obstruct every move you make.

I have written[3] our agent on the Pacific Coast to discuss with you the premiums on the different policies we offer.[4] I am sure he will be able to give you at least a partial list of names that will help you.

I imagine[5] the most difficult part of your job will be to convince people, in simple language, that they should carry insurance.[6] People feel persecuted when they are asked to insure their lives or their property. People offer all kinds[7] of ridiculous excuses for not buying an insurance policy. However, it is not so difficult[8] to sell insurance as it was a few years ago. At that time our company had just been established and[9] people had no assurance that it was financially sound. Sincerely yours, (193 standard words)

Dear Sir: I am sending you today a parcel containing material which gives the principal facts relative[1] to our new "practical insurance policy." This policy is very popular in the South, and I[2] imagine it will soon become popular in other parts of the country. The premiums for this policy[3] are very low. Sincerely yours, (65 standard words)

Dear Mr. Jones: The dress patterns which you enclosed in the parcel you sent us were badly torn. It is obvious[1] that the patterns were not carefully handled. As these patterns were the property of our best customer, we shall[2] have to ask you to make immediate adjustment.

I assume this damage occurred while the parcel was in the[3] hands of the post office, and if you could send us a certificate showing that the parcel was given to them[4] in good shape, we shall be glad to take care of the matter ourselves.

In the future, when it is necessary to[5] send patterns by mail, please be sure that they are carefully wrapped. Some of the patterns cannot satisfactorily[6] be duplicated. Cordially yours, (126 standard words)

Gentlemen: Thank you for your cooperation in sending us so promptly your check for $189.[1] This payment will enable us to fill the order of April 16 without further delay. No time[2] has been lost, as the shipment was packed and ready to be shipped when your check arrived.

As our organization carries[3] no accounts, I wonder if you would be good enough to enclose a check with each order. You realize that[4] we could not offer our goods at such low prices if we had to carry a large bookkeeping division. Cordially[5] yours, (101 standard words)

Assignment 48

227. Changes, publication, favorable, sooner, loved, collection, dealer, regarding, unnecessary, prepares, unprepared, opinions, ascend, asked, values, expresses, looked, billing, experiences, finds, lights.

228. Absent-absence, absolute, accomplish, appreciate-appreciation, association, attitude, benefit, cancel, corporation, enthusiasm, essential, frequent, indicate, journal, local, splendid, reciprocate, numerous, ordinary, specify, permanent, prominent, practice, render, separate, similar, social, title, total, territory.

229. Repetition, competition, station, quotation, notation, edition, addition, condition, foundation, commission, information, permission, intimation, definition, combination, recognition, destination.

230. Reading and Writing Exercise

TIMEPIECES

In a recent edition of a local journal I noticed a headline to an advertisement which read, "Clocks[1] for cattle." This title was so prominently displayed and so unusual that I proceeded to read the[2] whole advertisement. I discovered that it was a quotation from a letter dated 1816. The author[3] of this letter had indicated his intention to give a certain number of cattle in exchange for[4] a few clocks.

Although we would not today consider giving a cow for a clock, we must realize how[5] absolutely essential and prominent a part clocks play in our everyday lives. Numerous changes have been made since[6] the marvelous invention of the clock, but it still renders the same service to mankind—it tells us the time.

We[7] have definite information that clocks similar to ours were used in the ninth century, but they were found only[8] in the splendid homes of the wealthy. Today clocks are an absolute necessity in every home, and frequently[9] you will find three or four clocks in the poorest of homes. There was one important omission on the early[10] clocks—there was no minute hand to indicate the exact time. Later, the addition of the minute hand and still[11] later the second hand made it possible to determine accurately the time of the day.

In my estimation,[12] a clock is the most human of all furniture, especially the older clocks, made hundreds of years ago.[13]

The clocks manufactured in the factory can never take the place of those made by the old masters, who showed[14] their enthusiasm for their work by putting their whole heart and soul into it. The old master exercised great[15] care in the formation of each piece that went into the clock, and the separate parts were carefully put together.[16] There were no local stores in those days that handled the sale of clocks, and there was very little competition.[17] A man had to peddle his clocks from house to house until he covered the entire territory.

A person who[18] appreciates old clocks will enjoy examining the clock that is a prominent part of the home of our first[19] President. It stands in the hall and, without complaint, keeps ticking off the seconds, minutes and hours. A notation[20] was made on a sheet of paper in the clock, which gives the information that it was to be removed for repairs,[21] but that order must have been cancelled, as the repairs were not made. Frequently the clock loses a total of three[22] or four minutes, and that is the only intimation it gives of its age. But then, some watches that have just been[23] manufactured are not in as good condition and lose much more time than this. (473 standard words)

Dear Sir: I received permission from the local corporation to build a house on the vacant lot. The corporation[1] gave me this permission with the condition that the house must have a stone foundation. I can sympathize[2] with their attitude, and I know this stone foundation will be of benefit to all concerned.

If I am absent[3] from the office on Monday, I shall be in the commissioner's office making all the essential arrangements.[4]

The house will be in an ideal spot, just three blocks from the local station. The post office renders some splendid service[5] in this part of the town.

I hope to be able to begin work very soon. When I am ready, I shall get[6] in touch with you. Cordially yours, (125 standard words)

Assignment 49

231. Patrons, patterns, plaintiff, occupied, obstruct, practical, probability, estate, neglected, observed, negligent, mortgage, litigation, merchant, headquarters, legislation, likewise, independent-independence, indispensable, doctrine, English, freight, glorious, familiar, entitled.

232. Prosecute, publication, punctual, pupil, push, qualify, remainder, resignation, salesman, scarce, secretary, signature, significant-significance, silence, specify, specific.

233. *Any:* Anybody, anyone, anywhere, anyhow, anyway. *Be:* Before, beforehand, behindhand, belong, beside, besides. *Ever-y:* Whatever, whenever, whichever, however, whoever, everybody, everyone, everywhere. *Here:* Hereafter, herein, hereinafter, hereinbefore, hereon, hereto, heretofore, herewith. *There:* Thereafter, therein, therefore, therefrom, thereon, thereto, thereupon, therewith.

234. Reading and Writing Exercise

Dear Sir: On January 19 the manager sent his resignation to the secretary of our[1] organization. Mr. Brown, who had been a salesman for many years and who had charge of the publications issued[2] by this company, was appointed to fill the vacancy.

One of Mr. Brown's first actions was to put his[3] signature to a new lease. This new lease will provide the space we have needed for a long time. Besides the manager[4] and all the people belonging to his staff, everybody in the credit division will move to the new[5] quarters. The shipping division, however, will remain where it is. Heretofore all these divisions were on the[6] same floor, and the employees could scarcely move from desk to desk without pushing into somebody.

The next time your[7] salesman is in this territory, why not have him make it a specific point to come in to see our new offices?[8] Yours truly, (163 standard words)

Dear Sir: Your absence from our store for the past few months has been noted, and it has been a long time since we have received[1] any orders from you. We feel that this silence is a significant indication that you have become[2] dissatisfied with our service or our goods. As you used to be one of our best customers and friends, we are anxious[3] to have a talk with you and do whatever we can to regain your confidence.

If you will specify the[4] time that will be most convenient for you, I should like to have my secretary call on you and discuss the matter.[5] He will be there punctually at whatever time you set.

Herewith you will find an envelope for your[6] convenience in writing me when my secretary may see you. Yours truly, (132 standard words)

Dear Sir: After the unpleasant dealings which a number of our customers had in ordering our publications,[1] we have decided to send out a salesman for the remainder of the year.

Hereafter all orders will be[2] handled through the main office.

As you will recall, a man representing himself as one of our salesmen went through[3] your territory and made many liberal offers to pupils and their parents. He was no longer employed[4] by this organization, as his resignation had been demanded several months before. We knew nothing[5] about his actions, however, until our secretary started to receive letters stating that magazines[6] had not been received. As soon as we discovered what had happened, we asked every one to specify the publications[7] ordered, and we put all names on our mailing list. We are pushing charges against this man, and he will be[8] prosecuted. Now the matter has been settled to everybody's satisfaction. This sort of thing can happen[9] anywhere to anybody, and therefore we should be grateful that we were able to straighten matters before[10] anyone really suffered. Cordially yours, (207 standard words)

Dear Sir: Next month this country will celebrate Mark Twain's birthday, and we are planning to take part in the celebration.[1] In his honor, we are sponsoring an essay contest. We are calling on you as principal of the school[2] to cooperate with us. We should appreciate it very much if you would see that this is announced to all[3] the pupils in the school, as they will be the only ones qualified to write in this contest. The contest will be[4] announced beforehand in the daily papers and other publications, but pupils do not always read these[5] publications. Pupils will be given specific directions when they leave their signature and address at our office.[6] Anyone wishing to compete in the essay contest should be punctual and call on us soon. The secretary[7] will give each candidate all the necessary information. He will also give him a pamphlet containing[8] all the rules governing the contest.

The winner will receive a complete set of the works of Mark Twain. This[9] set will be a valuable addition to the library of any pupil. In addition to this main[10] prize, there will be two other fine prizes. The second prize winner will receive $10 in gold and the third prize winner a fountain[11] pen. All papers must be in our hands on the day specified in the rules. Yours truly, (235 standard words)

Assignment 50

235. Punctual, silence, secretaries, salesmen, publication, pushed, specify, resignation, practices, premium, property, parcel, neglect, litigation, husband, junior, estate, glorious.

236. *Where:* Whereabouts, whereas, wherever, wherefore, wherein, whereof, elsewhere. *Soever:* Whatsoever, Wheresoever, whensoever, whosoever, whomsoever. *Some:* Somebody, somehow, someone, sometime, somewhat, somewhere. *With:* Within, withstand, forthwith, notwithstanding. Meanwhile, otherwise, thanksgiving.

237. $5; 500; $500; 5,000; $5,000; 500,000; 5,000,000; $5,000,000, 5 lbs. (or £5); 500 lbs. (or £500); £5,000; £500,000; 5 gallons; 5 barrels; 5 bushels; 5 feet; 5 cwt.; 5 o'clock; 500 feet; 5 francs; 500 francs. A dollar; a pound; a million; a gallon; per hundred; several hundred; several hundred dollars; a thousand dollars; few thousand dollars; a hundred thousand.

238. Reading and Writing Exercise

Dear Sir: Thank you for your very frank letter of January

5 regarding your account with us for[1] $5,000. Everybody is up against it at some time or other. We have been ourselves. That is exactly[2] why we are going to help you.

Don't worry about that $5,000, even though it is somewhat past due.[3] Forget it for 90 days. Meanwhile, we are going to ask you to sign a note covering that period. If[4] you can pay it within that time, well and good. Our own financial condition is excellent, and a few thousand[5] dollars will not worry us particularly at this time.

We wouldn't do a favor like this for everyone,[6] but we know that you are all right. We want you to build up a good business, and we are going to help you.

It[7] is a pleasure to have people know that we sell service as well as merchandise. Just sign the note and return it[8] to us promptly. Yours truly, (163 standard words)

Dear Sir: Sometime ago someone in your office asked us the whereabouts of the salesman who sold your client[1] several thousand dollars' worth of machinery which turned out to be useless. At first we decided to have nothing[2] whatsoever to do with this case, but this same incident occurred again recently, and this time the victim[3] was one of our best friends. We are now determined to prevent similar occurrences, and we are willing[4] to offer $500 for information concerning the whereabouts of this individual.

We[5] received a letter from somebody in your city suggesting that he was somewhere in Chicago, but somehow[6] we could place little confidence in that information. We are convinced that he is elsewhere.

Our offer of[7] $500 was announced at three o'clock yesterday, and if necessary this offer will be increased to[8] $1,000. Sincerely yours, (166 standard words)

Dear Sir: Please ship immediately 300 feet of the steel wire advertised some time ago in the local[1] newspapers. I think the price mentioned at the time was $15 for 100 feet. Also, please ship 5 gallons[2] of the red paint about which I wrote you. This will cost about $3 a gallon and is guaranteed to[3] withstand the heat of the summer as well as the frost of the winter.

I should like to have all this material[4] before Thanksgiving, and if you can arrange to have it all here by that time, I shall greatly appreciate it.[5] Yours very truly, (103 standard words)

Dear Mr. Brown: From your letter of January 21 I think our recollection of the original[1] negotiations is about the same. The only discrepancy, in my judgment, is the one brought up by[2] the second and third paragraphs of your letter. Apparently, it is your impression that the question of caring[3] for daily mailings did not come up until after you had started on the job.

As a matter of fact, it[4] was this matter of caring for the daily mailings that brought the job to you several years ago. The mailer[5] who handled this work originally had done a good enough piece of work on mailing the magazines each month.[6] He could not, however, keep his records straight when it came to handling our daily mailings. Because of our[7] dissatisfaction with his method of handling the daily mailings, I started to look for someone else.

I find that you[8] now have on hand about 80,000 copies of our magazine. In accordance with our practice of paying[9] for the entire delivery at one time, we have been charged for the mailing of these 80,000 copies. These[10] 80,000 copies represent, at $2 a thousand, the considerable charge of $160,[11] for which we have received no return. In addition, these 80,000 copies are worth about[12] $100 in waste paper.

You can see that we cannot very well overlook this item, and I should[13] appreciate it if we could settle the matter before the end of this year, so that we may have our records straight.[14] Yours truly, (282 standard words)

Dear Sir: I have tried every way possible to convince myself that it would be all right for me to ship you the[1] 5,000 feet of lumber requested in your letter of January 8, but I simply can't do it until[2] you have been able to reduce your present open account.

I know you will be disappointed, but I do[3] not want you to feel at all hurt. It isn't a question of confidence in you— our past relations show that. It[4] just is not discreet in the present trade conditions, to carry an open account of more than $3,000[5] for a store doing your volume of business. Sincerely yours, (111 standard words)

Assignment 51

239. Specific, prosecute, publication, specify, pupil, push, qualify, silence, resignation, significant-significance, secretary, scarce, salesman, obvious, occupy-occupation, plaintiff, practical, premium, probability, property, partial, pattern, literary, merchant, misdemeanor, negligence, negotiate, messenger, passenger, manufacture, observe, inasmuch, independent-independence, likewise, jury, legislative, investigate, emphasize-emphasis, execute, freight, coupon, curious, commerce.

240. $8.50; 5 cents; 5 per cent; 5 per cent per annum.

241. Society, subsequent, substitute, succeed, sympathy, testimonial, testimony, text, unavoidable, universal, variety. verdict, vote, warehouse, wholesale, wife.

242. Reading and Writing Exercise

Dear Madam: The Universal Book Society is an organization that makes available to book[1] lovers a large variety of the latest and finest books. Each month we submit to the members of the[2] Universal Book Society a list of books that we consider outstanding. The members vote for the book they[3] would prefer for the month's selection, and the verdict of the voters governs our decision. If, for some reason,[4] the month's selection does not appeal to you, you may substitute another book from the list.

However, instead[5] of paying the regular price of $3.45 for the regular selection, you will have[6] to pay $4.95 for the substitution. The additional charge is due to the fact that[7] we can get the regular selection at a wholesale price from the warehouse, while we must pay the retail price for[8] the substitution. We are sure, though, that we shall succeed in pleasing you most of the time. If one book does not appeal[9] to you, subsequent books will.

The Universal Book Society allows a 5 per cent discount from the[10] $3.45 price to those who pay in advance for the entire year's books. In addition, we pay[11] the unavoidable 10 cents delivery charge.

The Universal Book Society has many prominent[12] members. If you will turn to page 10 of the enclosed booklet you will find there many testimonials from[13] famous people who are in entire sympathy with our ideas. As you will see, there is a testimonial[14] from the wife of a former President. Cordially yours, (290 standard words)

Dear Sir: We regret the unavoidable delay in bringing your case to trial. If all goes well, however, I[1] am sure we should be able to get all the testimony in and have the jury bring in a verdict. The judge[2] already has prepared the text of his charge to the jury. He has asked for a copy of the testimony,[3] which we are sending him today.

To be sure that nothing goes wrong, please bring with you all the necessary warehouse[4] receipts, so that we may present them while the testimony is being taken. Cordially yours, (97 standard words)

Dear Sir: In subsequent issues of our textbook we shall substitute a larger size of type for the one we are[1] now using. The type will be about 20 per cent larger. We are also reducing the price of the text from[2] $4.20 to $3.65. Our binder succeeded in getting a low wholesale[3] price on the binding cloth, and we are thus able to pass this saving along to our customers. We are in[4] complete sympathy with the feelings of our customers that the cost of texts should be reduced. Cordially yours, (99 standard words)

Dear Sir: We are sorry that the desk you ordered as a gift for your son arrived so badly damaged that you cannot[1] accept it. The railroad agent gave me a receipt acknowledging that the desk was received in perfect[2] condition from our warehouse. Therefore, it must have been damaged while in the possession of the railroad.

Although we cannot[3] be held responsible for the desk once it leaves our warehouse, we know you are anxious to give this desk to your[4] son, and we are, therefore, sending you today another desk exactly like the first one we sent you. It should reach[5] you promptly.

If you will telephone the express company to make a special delivery immediately[6] upon the arrival of the desk, you should have it just in time for your son's birthday.

Please leave the damaged desk[7] in the hands of the railroad company. We shall deal with them later.

Thank you for writing me so promptly. I assure[8] you our only desire is to see that you receive the desk in perfect condition. Sincerely yours, (178 standard words)

Dear Sir: This morning I received a letter from your wife giving me the date on which you will pay your account. I[1] appreciate your having her write me. The tone of the letter convinces me that you are honest, and that you[2] take pride in paying your debts. I know you will meet your obligation promptly.

I am enclosing a stamped envelope[3] for your convenience in making the payment when it is due. Cordially yours, (74 standard words)

CHAPTER X

Assignment 52

243. Careless, clears, listed, following, purchased, numbered, shipped, expected, unused, friendless, strongly, correction, communicates, efforts.

244. Actor, tractor, conductor, detector, protector. Effected, affected, detected, directed, selected. Active, detective, defective, attractive, effective, elective.

245. Have done, has been done, has done, will be done, would be done, should be done, could be done.

246. Quicker than, better than, sooner than, rather than, nearer than, greater than.

247. Give us, tell us, write us, to us, let us, mail us, wire us.

248. Credit department, shipping department, purchasing department, accounting department, mailing department, billing department.

249. Reading and Writing Exercise

Dear Sir: As the active head of the accounting department, I am calling a special meeting to see what can[1] be done about standardizing the reports of the salesmen who write us each week. Something must be done and should be[2] done immediately. I have received many complaints, not only from the members of the accounting department,[3] but from the heads of the shipping department, the mailing department, and the credit department, that the reports[4] are too long and do not give all the necessary facts. It is my thought that the man who selected the present[5] report blank was not familiar with the work of the accounting department and the other divisions of[6] our company. If he had been, he would have done a far more effective job.

I had originally planned to[7] hold this meeting in two weeks. However, in order that we may have something definite on which to work, I am[8] asking the managers of the different divisions to submit a blank that would eliminate the necessity[9] for their writing us and wiring us for information every time a report comes in. I think that almost[10] anything these men suggest will be better than what we now have.

I am writing this memorandum to you[11] because whatever will be done in the next few days will affect you more than it will affect any other branch[12] of the business. I think, though, that we are nearer than we have ever been to a solution. Cordially yours, (259 standard words)

Dear Madam: The man who stole your purse in the car last week was caught by the detective who was placed in charge of the[1] case. The detective had a long talk with the conductor of the car and then planned what should be done. The detective[2] directed several of his men to take up the search, and soon one of them detected a rough-looking fellow[3] who had a woman's purse sticking out of his pocket. When this fellow was arrested, he acted surprised, but he[4] was a poor actor, and a few minutes later he confessed.

Your purse is now in our possession, and if you will[5] mail us a note telling us exactly what was in the bag when it was stolen, we shall be glad to return the[6] bag to you.

The detective who had charge of your case has been selected for promotion, and beginning April[7] 15 he will be a captain. Because of his fine work in your case and many other similar cases, he[8] has earned the promotion and the attractive salary that goes with it. Yours truly, (175 standard words)

Dear Mr. Brown: I am sorry that the tractor which we shipped to you is defective. I have had our shipping[1] department trace this shipment, and I find that all parts were in excellent condition when they left us. We are writing[2] our Chicago office to send a man to your farm immediately, to see what can be done about getting[3] the tractor in good working condition again.

The demand for these tractors has been much greater than we expected,[4] and consequently our factory is working day and night to catch up. However, even though we are getting[5] out these tractors quicker than we have done at any previous time, the quality of the parts and the[6] workmanship has not decreased. In fact, our purchasing department has given us the best materials obtainable[7] for these tractors. Everything has been done to build the finest and most attractive tractor that can be made for[8] the lowest possible price. I think you will agree that in this respect our success has been greater than we could[9] possibly have hoped for.

We realize, of course, that it is not always possible for our friends on the farm to[10] pay cash for these tractors. Consequently, we have selected a man to take charge of our credit department who[11] has had years of experience on the farm, a man who is in sympathy with the problems of the farmer. He[12] has done a great deal in solving the financial problems of the farmer.

I am confident that our man will be[13] able to repair your tractor without too much difficulty, but to be sure that everything turns out all right,[14] we are asking him to let us have a full report of his visit with you. In the meantime, if we can assist[15] you in any way, please be sure to write to us. Sincerely yours, (311 standard words)

Dear Sir: Please accept my personal thanks for the new checking account which you were good enough to open with us[1] today. We appreciate your business, and I know our relations will be beneficial to both of us.

As[2] you know, we have a savings department for those who care to open such an account. Our safe deposit department[3] has a private safe in its vaults ready for your use whenever you need this type of service. Our real estate[4] department is also well equipped to take care of all your real estate business.

We feel that as a depositor[5] of ours you are entitled to the best service which can be rendered you by every member of our institution.⁶ We hope you will write us freely and frequently. On our part, we shall try to see that your relations here⁷ are so pleasant that you will not only be satisfied, but pleased—pleased so well that you will recommend our bank to⁸ your friends when the occasion arises. Yours truly, (169 standard words)

ASSIGNMENT 53

250. Accommodations, authoritative, automobile, bureau, Atlantic, affidavit, American, application, compare, commercial, conversation, conspicuous, citizens, connection, default, disappoint, discuss, distinct-distinction, energy.

251. Of course, at once, at any rate, great deal, I always, on hand, as follows, whole lot, one another, day's sight, do you know, great pleasure, your order, first class, whether or not, at all events, to some extent, to a great extent, to such an extent, at the same time, in other words, once in a while, in my opinion, in the first place, as soon as possible, as a matter of fact, on account of the fact, over and over again.

252. A.m., p.m., C.O.D., price list, list price, vice versa, bank draft, order blank, Associated Press, Democratic party, Republican party, New York Central, Illinois Central, selling price, market price, Union Pacific, Great Britain, enclosed blank, General Manager, Assistant General Manager, indemnity policy, Canadian Pacific, application blank, bond and mortgage, Federal Reserve Board, certificate of deposit, Chamber of Commerce.

253. Reading and Writing Exercise

Dear Sir: Your order was received by the general manager

at 9 a.m. this morning. At 3 p.m. the[1] general manager turned your order over to the assistant general manager who has charge of such[2] orders.

The assistant general manager, however, could not fill your order at once, because, in the first[3] place, he did not know whether you wanted the goods sent direct to the Chamber of Commerce Building or to the Board of Education Building. Once in a while the school board prefers to have material of this kind[1] sent C.O.D.[5]

In the second place your order did not give all the necessary information. To be sure that we get[6] all the necessary information, the general manager asked me to send you our order blank as soon[7] as possible. As a matter of fact, every few days we receive orders which do not give all the necessary[8] information, and therefore we have arranged the enclosed blank in such a way that it will, to a great extent,[9] eliminate errors. The order blank provides a space for the selling price, the market price, as well as the list[10] price.

At the same time there is a column in which you can check whether or not you want the goods sent by first class mail,[11] or whether you prefer to have them sent C.O.D. In my opinion, this order blank saves a great deal of time.[12]

Of course, we are anxious to hear from you at once, and therefore we are enclosing a stamped envelope for your reply.[13] Cordially yours, (263 standard words)

Dear Friend: Each year the Democratic party, the Republican party, and other political parties, send[1] out literature giving their views on the major campaign issues. I always read this literature very[2] carefully. As a member of the Federal Reserve Board, I must keep up to date with the attitudes of these[3] political parties toward the stock market, the curb market, and other financial institutions. In other[4] words, I must be familiar with what they would do if they were elected to office.

A great deal of the literature[5] must be studied carefully. On account of the fact that all literature of this nature does not give[6] the true facts, it is wise to read all available material on the subject in the newspapers. The[7] Associated Press gives accurate information on the attitudes of the political parties. The Board[8] of Management of the Associated Press has said over and over again that it will release no[9] information that has not been verified. At any rate, I have on hand a letter from the chairman of the[10] board assuring me of this. I have personally found the reports of the Associated Press to be accurate[11] in every detail. Cordially yours, (227 standard words)

Dear Sir: Do you know a good insurance company that would be willing to send me some printed literature[1] on the endowment policies and the indemnity policies they issue? I have, to some extent, made up[2] my mind to take out a policy, and if the insurance company will enclose an application blank, I[3] shall be glad to take it into consideration.

It is my impression that some organizations will not[4] accept the application blank of a man who does a great deal of flying. I do a whole lot of traveling[5] on the New York Central, the Baltimore & Ohio, and the Illinois Central, but I do very little[6] flying. I seldom use the Canadian Pacific and the Northern Pacific, as my organization[7] does little business with the sections covered by those railroads. Once in a while business takes me to Great Britain, but[8] this does not happen often.

I am asking several other people to send me information

on the subject[9] of insurance. When I have had an opportunity to see what all the different insurance companies[10] have to offer, I shall take great pleasure in discussing the matter with the agent of the company I[11] select. Until that time, of course, I can take no action. Yours very truly, (233 standard words)

Dear Sir: We shall be glad to open a credit account for you and give you full credit privileges. The[1] information we have received concerning you is so completely favorable to you personally and as[2] a business man that we appreciate your choosing us to supply you with the goods you need. Your order is[3] going forward today.

As general manager of this company, I assure you of our complete cooperation[4] at all times and of our efforts to help you realize greater profits through the sale of your goods.

We have[5] packed with your order our latest assortment of window display cards, with full directions how to make the display[6] attractive. At stated intervals, you will hear from our business promotion department, which is conducted solely[7] for our customers.

If, at any time, there is anything this organization can do for you, I should[8] consider it a personal favor if you will write direct to me. Never have the slightest hesitation[9] in writing us. Cordially yours (185 standard words)

Assignment 54

254. Drill on Previous Assignments. Avoid, exercise, civil, clerk, compare, comparative, conclude, conclusion, connect, disappoint, familiar, likewise, independent, indispensable, observe, pattern, remainder, significant-significance, wholesale, specify, partial, practical, probability, property, litigation, legislation, literature.

255. Incl-. Incline, inclined, inclination, include, includes, included, including, inclusion, inclusive.

256. -ciency. Deficiency, efficiency, proficiency.

257. -ship. Authorship, fellowship, friendship, guardianship, hardship, leadership, membership, ownership, relationship, steamship, township, warship, apprenticeship.

258. Post-. Postage, postal, postman, postmark, postmaster, post office, postpone, postponed, post card.

259. Circu-. Circulate, circulated, circulation, circuit, circular, circulars, circus.

206. Intr-. Introduce, introduced, introduces, introduction, introductory, intrude, intruded, intrusion, intricate, intrigue.

Reading and Writing Exercise

261. Dear Sir: We appreciate your letter of December 2 regarding your dissatisfaction with the suite[1] *included* with the lot of furniture that you purchased from us some time ago and that was delivered just before[2] Thanksgiving.

This suite was *included* with a shipment that we purchased from a local bankrupt factory, and the[3] *workmanship* and quality do not represent our regular grade of merchandise. It may be that the *deficiencies*[4] you mention could be satisfactorily remedied, but we are *inclined* to believe that you would be[5] better satisfied if you were to exchange this suite for something from our regular line, the quality of which[6] we could absolutely guarantee.

If you will stop in to see us the next time you are in town, we will make proper[7] adjustment. We appreciate the value of a customer's good will, and we have no *inclination* to[8] expect you to keep a purchase that does not prove at least reasonably satisfactory. We are more concerned[9] about maintaining our *leadership* in the business life of this *township* than we are in forcing on you the[10] *ownership* of furniture the *deficiencies* of which we recognize. Very truly yours, (215 standard words) (First occurrence: *incl-, -ciency, -ship.*)

262. Dear Sir: Thank you for returning the *post card* attached to our recent *circular*.

It is a pleasure to *include*[1] samples of several tapestries, from which we hope you will be able to make selections for an *introductory*[2] order.

We are also glad to *include* with this letter a copy of our latest catalogue, which is[3] not yet in general *circulation,* and which contains all our prices on furniture.

The *inclusion* of the[4] *circulars* will give you a good *introduction* to these tapestries. I am *inclined* to believe that our *proficiency*[5] in the weaving of these tapestries, combined with the technical *efficiency* of our mills, will make it[6] possible for you to get these goods from us cheaper than from any other source of supply. Because of your[7] *membership* in the Consumers' League, you probably know that the prices are *inclusive* of postage but that the special[8] discount sale for members has been *postponed* because of the *deficiency* in our present looms. This *deficiency*[9] will be remedied within a week or two, as we are preparing for the *inclusion* in our working unit[10] of the looms from Erie.

It will be gratifying to receive your order. Yours very truly, (217 standard words) (First occurrence: *post-, circu-, intr-.*)

263. Dear Sir: The invoice covering your shipment of sporting goods was mailed to you yesterday.

We can furnish you with[1] the product that you asked about in any quantity. The regular price of this item is $75,[2] but when it is ordered in quantities of ten or more, we make the special price of $70. If[3] ordered in still larger quantities, we can quote you still lower terms.

Please send us your order as soon as possible,[4] as we do not know how long this price will be in effect. Very truly yours, (94 standard words)

264. Gentlemen: Please send to our Houston branch 25 crates of grapefruit, 50 crates of oranges, and 60 crates[1] of lemons.

Your *circular* letter says that we are entitled to a 5 per cent discount, so please bear this in[2] mind. Very truly yours, (44 standard words)

265. RELAX

It is good for you to relax, to be frivolous, and to let a spirit of fun run riot for a time.[1] Being always dignified causes stagnation of the mind, while a play spirit helps you to do your work. A task is[2] lighter for the heart's being light.

Neither mind nor body can be kept constantly under tension without impairing[3] its usefulness.

The spirit of play keeps one young. Many a trifling annoyance can be turned into a[4] humorous incident by a merry heart that has readiness to see the amusing side of things. A happy,[5] cheerful temper promotes good health, and good health promotes a happy, cheerful temper. Don't be afraid of seeming foolish[6] when you play.

The more serious your occupation, the heavier your cares, the more you need a play spell. However[7] great you may be, however important your occupation, forget them both for a time. Let yourself loose from[8] the tension of cares and become a child in spirit. You will live longer and do better work. (176 standard words)

266. Drill on Previous Assignments.   Include, efficiency, citizenship, partnership, postal, postponed, circulation, circulated, introduced, introduces, incline, inclined, included.

267. Inter-. Interest, interests, interested, interfere, interference, interior, internal, internally, international, interrupt, interruption, intersection, interstate, interval, intervene, interview, intermission, uninteresting, disinterested.

268. Destr-, distr-. Destroy, destroyed, distress, distribute, distributed, distributor, distribution, district, destruction, destructive.

269. Centr-.   Center, centered, central, centrally, centralize, centralization, concentrate, concentrated, concentration.

270. Short-, ship-. Short, shortage, shorter, shortest, shorten, shortly, shorthand, shortsighted, shipload, shipwreck, shipyard.

Reading and Writing Exercise

271. Gentlemen: The men and the letters that make contacts between your firm and your customers should dress the part. For[1] every *interview* credited to a salesman, scores of calls are made by your business correspondence and *circulars*.[2] A well-groomed letter or *circular* commands respect and *interest*.

Your message on a *Postal* Bond letterhead,[3] enclosed in a *Postal* Bond envelope, does you justice. It cultivates the *friend-*

ship of your customers and confirms[4] your *leadership*. Every-where in America, the famous *Postal* Bond watermark stands for the best. And business[5] leaders, recognizing the fact, *include* the name *Postal* Bond in giving orders for their fine stationery and[6] permanent records. *Postal* Bond does not *intrude* on the customer's notice. It does not *interfere* with the[7] *efficiency* of your carefully written letter or *circular*. It serves as the medium by which the thought is[8] conveyed to the reader without *interruption*—and that is always the proper *relationship* of the paper[9] and the printing.

"*Interpreting* the Modern Trend in Letterheads" is the title of a new portfolio,[10] containing valuable ideas for business stationery. We shall be very glad to send you a copy. Yours[11] truly, (221 standard words) (First occurrence: *inter-*.)

272. Dear Sir: Have you made your will?

Court records show that one of every two persons who die leaving an estate has made[1] no will.

It is important that every man make a will, because if he does not, he is forcing the state to[2] *interfere* in the *distribution* of his property. Laws change frequently—laws in various states are different.[3] The statutes seldom *distribute* his property as he would have it *distributed* were he handling the matter[4] himself.

Whether you have made a will or not you will be *interested* in reading a booklet entitled "Don't[5] *Postpone* Your Will," which has just been published as a service to policyholders in the *Central* Union Life[6] Insurance Company.

On receipt of the enclosed card we will be pleased to send you a complimentary copy.[7] No *postage* is required on the enclosed *post card,* and there is no obligation involved in making this[8] request. We should like this to serve as your *introduction* to the service of the *Central Union* Life Insurance[9] Company to its clients in this *district*. Sincerely, (190 standard words) (First occurrence: *distr-, centr-.*)

273. Dear Mr. Green: Hard work ceases to be hard work when one loves it. One must work for the love of it to succeed in[1] it. To make a success in any profession one must work, and work *uninterruptedly,* with both mind and[2] body, but chiefly with the mind.

The importance of keeping one's profession or aim constantly in the mind cannot[3] be too strongly emphasized. The path is long and straight and narrow, with no side paths. *Concentrated* preparation[4] in school will save or *shorten* many a rocky road in later years.

Take the *short cut* now instead of looking for[5] one later on. Be sure that you can do anything that anyone else can do. Realize that if you don't do[6] it, somebody else will, and nobody will mourn your elimination from the contest. It is just like any[7] other contest—winners and losers. You have just as good a chance as anyone else to be *included* in that[8] *short* list of winners!

Make your choice now. There is just as much, and more, opportunity today. There never was a[9] *shortage* of opportunity. Don't *postpone* your success. One may as well be a success at twenty-five as at[10] fifty. The early training and *concentration* of the mind do the work. Yours truly, (215 standard words) (First occurrence: *short-.*)

274. Gentlemen: The credit rating that you asked for in your credit inquiry letter No. 231[1] has been investigated.

We find that this person is considered a "good credit risk" up to the amount[2] of $1,000. He does not abuse his privilege and has always paid promptly.

We are glad to serve you[3] in any way possible. Yours truly, (67 standard words)

275. Gentlemen: Some time ago we wrote you requesting a duplicate copy of your invoice dated November[1] 1, amounting to $24.25. We also sent you a shipper's form to fill in and[2] return to us, so that we might file a claim for damages received in your freight shipment to us of November 1.[3]

Please give this your prompt attention, as the time in which we may file claim is limited. Yours very truly, (78 standard words)

Assignment 56

276. Drill on Previous Assignments. Interview, district, destroyed, central, centerpiece, shortcomings, shipwreck, interfered, introduction, circulate, postage, fellowship, hardship, proficiency, included.

277. Under-. Underneath, undersell, undersigned, underestimate, underline, underscore, underground, undercurrent, undertake, undertook, understand, understood, misunderstand, misunderstood, I understand, we understood, they cannot understand, I do not understand.

278. Over-. Overcome, overestimate, overtime, overcharge, overcoat, overdraw, moreover.

279. Aggr-. Agree, agreed, agrees, agreeable, agreement, disagree, aggregate, aggressive, aggravate.

280. Para-. Paralyze, paradise, paragraph, parallel, paradox, paraffin, paramount, parasite.

281. Contr-. Control, controlled, controller, contract, contracted, contractor, contradict, contradicted, contrary, contribute, contribution, contributor, contributed, controversy.

Reading and Writing Exercise

282. Dear Sir: Confirming our conversation, we shall be glad to furnish you approximately 40,000, 8[1] by 16 solid cinder blocks at 24¼ cents each, delivered on the above-named job, subject[2] to 5 per cent discount, 10 days.

It is understood that 75 per cent of the payments are to be cash[3] each week, these payments to be made and guaranteed by the *Contractors* Title and Trust Company. In a letter[4] received today, the Trust Company *agrees* to this arrangement.

It is *further understood* that the deferred[5] payments of 25 per cent are to be paid by the *contractor's* notes drawn in your favor and indorsed by you to[6] us. These notes are due not later than thirty days after the last shipment, and are to be drawn for not *over*[7] ninety days. This renewal period is to bear *interest* at 6 per cent.

It is further *agreed* between us[8] that you are to assign to us a sufficient number of houses, the equity of which is held for you by[9] the *Contractors* Title and Trust Company, to cover the amount of notes mentioned in the preceding *paragraph*.[10]

There has been no exact *parallel* to this arrangement in our business dealings with you but the Trust Company's[11] fear of a possible *overdraft* has been *overcome* by this *agreement*. It will, they feel, give them *control*[12] of the *distribution* of the receipts and avoid any chance that you might *overestimate* your income and[13] *underestimate* your costs with a consequent attempt on your part to *overdraw* your account with them.

This will[14] act as a *contract* between us. If acceptable, please indicate your *agreement* by signing on the blank line[15] at the bottom of this letter. Very truly yours, (309 standard words) (First occurrence: *under-, over-, aggr-, para-, contr-*.)

283. Gentlemen: Last week I purchased a suit at your store and paid cash for it. It did not fit exactly, so I left[1] it for alterations. You were to have it sent to me the following day.

It came today, but there was a C.[2]O.D. of $45 on it. Correct this mistake and send the suit to me without further delay.[3] Very truly yours, (62 standard words)

284. Gentlemen: We thank you for your remittance in payment of our invoice of December 20, which we are[1] receipting and returning to you. We are enclosing some order blanks for your convenience in ordering additional[2] supplies in the future.

We promise you that any orders received by us will be filled promptly. Very[3] truly yours, (62 standard words)

285. Dear Mr. Guthrie: Upon investigating your credit standing we find you to be what we term a "very[1] good risk."

We shall be glad to extend credit to you, and cordially invite you to visit our store at your[2] earliest convenience. Let's get acquainted.

I am sure our business *relationships* will be entirely satisfactory.[3] Very truly yours, (65 standard words)

286. Dear Sir: I hold for collection against you the balance due, including interest, on a note, signed by you on[1] August 25, of this year, to E. B. Lowe and Son, for $91.50.

Before proceeding[2] further in the matter, I am giving you an opportunity to pay the note without suit, with its added[3] costs and inconveniences.

Please let me hear from you as soon as possible. Very truly yours, (77 standard words)

287. Safety

An improper idea of the safety of airplane travel is obtained through the unfortunate fact that the[1] average citizen hears only of the crashes and fatalities and very little, if anything, of the[2] thousands upon thousands of miles flown without any accident whatsoever.

The reliability of[3] the airways for safe transportation is well illustrated when one considers that merchandise insurance rates[4] from London to various European cities carry a preferential rate of from 70 to 35[5] per cent less than rates obtaining for surface transportation.

Although statistics on safety may have little[6] effect upon the air-mindedness of some individuals, yet it is quite interesting to note that for[7] every crash many thousands of miles have been flown with complete safety. (151 standard words)

288. Dear Sir: I regret, more than these few words will express, to be forced to answer the roll call in this manner. My[1] absence from this meeting is unavoidable, and the loss is mine. Is it necessary to say, "Count on me next[2] time"? Regretfully yours, (44 standard words)

Assignment 57

289. Drill on Previous Assignments. Control, parallel, disagree, oversight, undervalue, shortest, concentrate, distribution, international, intruder, circular, postmark, authorship, deficiency, inclination, disinclination, efficiency, ownership, postpone, internal, destructively, center, shortsighted, underscore, overestimate, aggravate, paragraph, contrary.

290. -sure. Assure, assured, assures, leisure, measure,

measurement, measurable, pressure, treasure, disclosure, exposure, composure, commensurate.

291. -ward, -hood. Backward, awkward, forward, upward, downward, homeward, onward, reward, boyhood, manhood, neighborhood, likelihood, falsehood, brotherhood.

292. Trans-. Transfer, transact, transacted, transaction, transform, translate, transmit, transplant, transport, transportation, transparent.

293. Super-, supr-. Superintend, superb, supervise, supervision, superficial, superfluous, supreme, suppress, suppressed.

294. -ure. Failure, figure, endure, procure, secure, securely, nature, picture, lecture, fixture, furniture, feature, mixture, capture, creature, departure, expenditure, adventure, overture.

295. -quire. Acquire, acquires, acquired, acquirement, inquire, inquires, require, requires, requirement.

Reading and Writing Exercise

296. Gentlemen: A *short* time ago, in response to an ever-increasing *pressure* from our *distributors,* we[1] printed color charts for the standard colors on the Puritan and Plymouth models.

Very frequently, we receive[2] letters from *distributors* and dealers complaining that they are unable to answer the question, "What are the[3] standard color combinations on the different models?"

Of course, this question may be vaguely answered by[4] referring to the cars as finished in brown or blue or whatever the color may be. And in most cases, even[5] if the terms *"Postal* gray" or *"Paradise* blue" were used, the customer would still have no conception of the colors,[6] because it is always hard to *measure* colors in words. That's where these timely little fold-ers fit in. They not[7] only give the names of the various colors but they also contain samples. These samples enable the cus-tomer[8] to examine the colors at his *leisure* and to *assure* him-self that he is getting exactly the[9] color combination he desires.

Included with a *circular* letter, the chart can be used as a mailing piece[10] to a list of customers. Attractively priced at 3 cents each, the charts should be ordered in quantities *com-mensurate*[11] with your needs. The blank will be found in the back of the booklet enclosed in this package. Very truly yours,[12] (240 standard words) (First occurrence: *-sure*.)

297. Gentlemen: Thank you for your order for one gross of handbags.

After checking our records, we find that we have[1] in stock at present only one-half gross of the style you wish. Rather than delay the shipment, we are sending you[2] one-half gross by express today. The rest will go *forward* within a few days, in all likelihood, although we may not[3] be able to send them until Monday. We appreciate this opportunity to *introduce* these handbags[4] in your *neighborhood*, and we are really *dis-tressed* that we are unable to fill your order completely.

We hope[5] that handling your order in this manner will not seriously inconvenience you. Yours very truly, (118 standard words) (First occurrence: *-hood, -ward*.)

298. FOLLOW OUT A PLAN

He who every morning plans the *transactions* of the day and follows out that plan carries a thread that will guide him[1] through the most busy life. The orderly *distribution* of his time is like a ray of light which darts itself through[2] all his occupations. But where no plan is laid, where the use of time is surrendered merely to chance, all things lie[3] huddled together in one *awkward* muddle, which admits of neither *distribution* nor review. *Victor Hugo.* (77 standard words) (First occurrence: *trans-.*)

299. AN ARTIST

Almost anybody can do business fairly well. Many men can do business very well. A few can do[1] business *superbly* well. But the man who not only does his work *superbly* well but adds to it the personal touch[2] through great zeal, patience, and persistence, *transforming* it into something unique, individual,[3] distinct, and unforgettable, is an artist. *Elbert Hubbard.* (67 standard words) (First occurrence: *super-.*)

300. Dear Sir: Today we received your shipment of cream, for which we thank you. We hope that you will be well pleased with your[1] returns. If for any reason you are not entirely pleased, be sure to write us and let us know, because we are anxious[2] to correct any mistake we may make.

If you happen to know any other cream producers who you think[3] might be interested in *securing* more for their cream, please give us their names. Yours very truly, (77 standard words) (First occurrence: *-ure.*)

301. Gentlemen: We regret to learn from your letter of November 14 that the tubes recently sent you were not[1] of the correct size. We have meanwhile *forwarded* 1 gross of our No. 165 test tubes, 7[2] by 7/8 inches, which we hope will answer your *requirements.*

Credit for the apparatus was issued[3] on November 18 and has undoubtedly been received at the present time.

Immediately upon[4] receipt of the test tubes you are returning to us, credit will be issued in full.

We are now making an *inquiry*[5] which will soon result in
the *disclosure* of the reasons for this *interference* with the usual
efficiency[6] of our *Distributing* Department. I hope these *awkward* errors will not interrupt the pleasant business[7] *relationship* which has existed between us for so many years, and I
am inclined to think that we have now[8] eliminated any chance
that such errors may occur again.

Thank you for this opportunity of[9] serving you. Yours very
truly, (185 standard words) (First occurrence: *-quire*.)

<h3 style="text-align:center">Assignment 58</h3>

302. Drill on Previous Assignments. Acquire, failure,
capture, superior, transformation, reward, likelihood, treasure,
contribute, paralyze, aggressive, overpaid, understood, ship-
builder, centralized, distribute, interminable, introduced, circuit, post card, membership, proficiency, inclusion, township,
intersection, shortage, underline, overjoyed, exposure, forward,
superlative, fixture, secure.

303. -ograph. Photograph, photographs, photographed,
photography, photographic, photographically, biography, biog-
rapher, geography, lithography, stenography, phonograph,
mimeograph, autograph, geographical.

304. -cal, -cle. Medical, chemical, logical, classical, economical, radical, typical, musical, physical, practical, periodical,
article, spectacle, vehicle, particle, chronicle.

306. -sult. Consult, consulted, consultation, insult, insult-
ed, insults, result, results, resultant.

306. -gram, -grim. Telegram, cablegram, diagram, program, pilgrim.

Reading and Writing Exercise

307. Gentlemen: Enclosed is a signed copy of the *contract* and *agreement* for a 5,000-pack order of[1] special business cards, given by you to our representative.

We understand that you desire to get the cards[2] before your *departure* on your spring trip through the *central* states.

Sketches for the various special *features* of this[3] card will be submitted for your approval promptly. I am *inclined* to feel that it would be better not to use[4] *pictures* of your *fixtures* because the *mixture* of type and *pictures* would spoil the appearance of the cards. Yours very[5] truly, (101 standard words)

308. Gentlemen: Let's get right after spring orders.

A few minutes of your time spent in revising the mailing list we[1] used last season will probably mean many early orders.

Just cross off the names of those whom we can no longer[2] *interest*—and don't fail to add all the newcomers!

The advertising this spring is the finest[3] ever, but success or *failure* depends entirely on the accuracy of your list.

We know you will take care of it very[4] promptly. The first lists we receive will be the first to be taken care of.

Thank you! Yours truly, (96 standard words)

309. Gentlemen: We shall soon place an order for 50,000 letterheads similar to the one on which this[1] letter is written.

Please quote us your best price on a lot of 50,000, *lithographed* on 20-pound bond paper.[2]

Please write me whether you think the *lithographic* process will enable you to manufacture these letterheads[3] any cheaper than you could make them if you print them from type. You should be able to save money if you use[4] *lithography* because then you can *photograph* my present letterhead, without having to set any type.

My[5] *stenographer* has asked me to warn you that these letterheads must be printed on a paper suitable for[6] *mimeograph*
work, as we use the *mimeograph* a great deal in our office.

When we come to an *agreement* as[7] to the method of printing and the prices, please submit a carbon copy. Yours truly,
(155 standard words) (First occurrence: -*ograph.*)

310. Gentlemen: From the enclosed *article* we learn that
pencils are to be manufactured from one of your by-products.[1]

We are penholder manufacturers, and we should like to
learn whether your material could be used[2] satisfactorily in
making penholders.

As we have no equipment here for *chemical* work, your
material[3] would have to reach us in such condition that it can
be used with *practically* no change. From reading the[4] *article*
I should judge that your material would be *economical* as well
as *practical*. If this is the[5] case, your sales should be large, because our work is *typical* of the work done in scores of similar
factories.[6] Therefore, it is *logical* to think that if we can use it
economically all these other factories could[7] also find it
economical.

It would be a pleasure to hear from you. If you are not yet
ready to[8] consider this suggestion, we hope that you will let us
hear from you when you are ready. Yours very truly, (178
standard words) (First occurrence: -*cle.*)

311. Dear Sir: We have been waiting to have our reports
and records brought up to date, so that we might inform you
of the[1] *results* of the *telegrams* sent out through your office,
soliciting aid for the *distressed* flood sufferers in your[2] *district*.

Of course, the local papers threw open their columns with
great kindness for the cause, and the[3] *telegrams* sent out right

after the country began to realize the enormity of the disaster had[4] splendid pulling power. To be exact, out of the 116 *telegrams* sent, we received exactly[5] 100 direct returns, and we are constantly getting additional *contributions*.

These *telegrams*[6] were naturally sent to a very select list, and their *contributions* represented approximately[7] one-third of the donations to the good cause.

There was no organization, no other solicitation,[8] except these *telegrams* and the newspaper *articles* mentioned above.

We are highly gratified with the part[9] the *telegrams* played in impressing upon the public the need of quick action. When you have time, I should like to[10] have an opportunity to *consult* with you about a *program* of further work along these lines. Apparently[11] by *concentrating* on a small list of those *inclined* to help persons in *distress* we can always hope for similar[12] results. Very truly yours, (245 standard words) (First occurrence: *-sult, -gram.*)

Assignment 59

312. Drill on Previous Assignments. Telegram, consult, historical, photography, acquired, natural, supervision, translation, falsehood, measure, contributor, parasite, aggregate, overflow, undersigned, shortly, concentrated, distress, interior, intruded, circulation, postman, leadership, deficiency, including.

313. -spect. Expect, expectation, inspect, inspection, inspector, prospect, prospective.

314. Electr-. Electric, electrical, electrician, electrify, electric light, electric wiring.

315. -city, -sity. Capacity, intensity, electricity, generosity, scarcity, immensity, publicity, velocity, curiosity, animosity, authenticity, audacity.

316. ual. Annual, annually, gradual, gradually, continual, continually, equal, unequal, effectual, actual, mutual, perpetual.

Reading and Writing Exercise

317. Gentlemen: Your *inquiry* of December 8, asking for further details in regard to the *Practical*[1] system of *electric* floor maintenance, is appreciated.

Practical machines are used with *equal efficiency*[2] to scrub, polish, and refinish all types of floors and floor coverings. There are eight models of *Practical* machines,[3] each different in price, design, *capacity,* and size—a *Practical* machine for your *requirements,* suited[4] to your floor area.

May we have some additional information as to your floor conditions, type of floors,[5] and *electric* current. The enclosed card is for this purpose. If you will give us this information, we can then[6] prepare a *schedule* for you based on your *actual* floor conditions. This *schedule* will convince you that our *electric* machines[7] will *gradually* pay for themselves, because the *annual* upkeep is so low. Yours very truly, (157 standard words) (First occurrence: *electr-, -city, -ual.*)

318. Gentlemen: Since our last letter to you we have decided to separate the East Coast into four distinct[1] territories.

The state of Maine is to be one of these territories, and a dealer at Portland[2] will be appointed to handle all *transactions* there.

Before we present our *proposal* to you, we should like very[3] much to have you answer the following questions:

1. Have you space for the storage of repair parts,[4] and pos-

sibly a consigned shovel, fully equipped and ready for immediate shipment to prospects in your[5] territory?

2. How many salesmen have you, and are they covering
the entire state of Maine?

3. How[6] long have you been selling to *contractors*?

This information will enable us to present you with our
dealer[7] *contract* for consideration.

Our dealer *contract* provides a very substantial commission
on the sale of[8] each machine, a 10 per cent commission on all
repair parts sold within the territory, and a liberal[9] policy of
advertising to all *prospects* in the territory.

We have *introduced* our machines[10] into eight states in the
short space of three months, and all machines placed thus far
are producing splendid records and[11] creating an *interest* that
indicates a considerable volume of business in the territories
they[12] reach.

We are now in a position to manufacture shovels and cranes
at the rate of one a day, thus *assuring*[13] you of shipments on
the same day that orders are received.

May we hear from you promptly? Yours very truly, (278
standard words) (First occurrence: *-spect*.)

319. Dear Sir: Did you ever arrange to meet somebody
downtown at exactly two o'clock and then hustle down there[1]
at exactly the right time only to find your friend among the
missing? If you have ever done that, standing first[2] on one
foot and then on the other while you searched your brain to
remember whether it really was two o'clock and[3] whether it
really was that particular street corner on which you had
agreed to meet—then you can appreciate[4] what we have just
gone through.

Last year we sold you coal, yet this fall when the first cold winds began whistling around the[5] corners and the telephone began to ring all day long with people wanting more of that fine coal we sell, we have[6] had no order from you.

To tell you the truth, we are all rather worried here at the office. Every one of us,[7] from the person who took your order over the telephone to the driver who delivered your coal, tried to give[8] the kind of service you wanted to have.

And now it is past the middle of January and another year[9] has started, and we have not had any order from you. We considered you one of the family and had hopes[10] of meeting you every fall and winter. So here we are waiting on the corner, so to speak, and we shall be[11] *overjoyed* to see you or to hear from you. Very cordially yours, (231 standard words)

320. Gentlemen: Your representative called on us recently and told us about the new burlap bag you are now[1] offering to the trade at greatly reduced prices. He left several samples with us.

We have been so greatly[2] impressed with the stock in the samples that we wish to enter our order for 10,000 bags, printed similar[3] to our order of September 30.

We shall have our purchasing department issue an order covering[4] this, and shall appreciate it greatly if you will rush this shipment along.

Please acknowledge receipt of this letter.[5] Yours very truly, (104 standard words)

Special Forms

173.

184.

194.

201.

211.

217.

220.

225.

232.

241.

CHART OF BRIEF FORMS

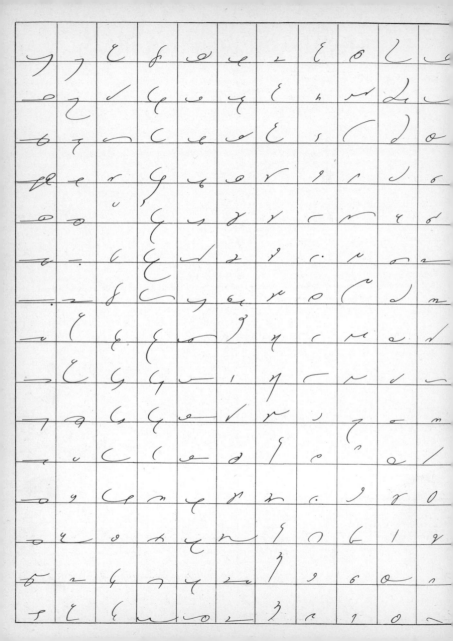

MOST-USED PHRASES

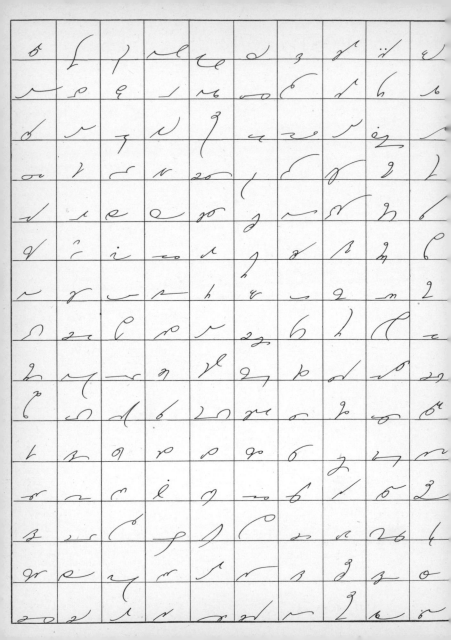